D0455360

Art Center College of Design
Library
1700 Lida Street
Pasadena, Calif. 91103

Monk

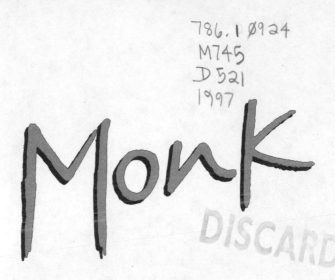

Monk

Laurent de Wilde

Translated by

Jonathan Dickinson

Marlowe & Company
New York

Published by
Marlowe & Company
632 Broadway, Seventh Floor
New York, NY 10012

Originally published in French as *Monk*
© Editions GALLIMARD, Paris, 1996.
Translation by Jonathan Dickinson © 1997 by Marlowe & Company.

Library of Congress Cataloging-in-Publication Data
De Wilde, Laurent.
[Monk. English]
Monk / by Laurent De Wilde; translated by Jonathan Dickinson.
p. cm.
Translation of: Monk.
ISBN 1-56924-740-4 (paper)
1. Monk, Thelonious.   2. Jazz musicians—United States—Biography.
I. Title.
ML417.M846D4213   1997
786.2'165'092—dc21
[B]   97-36668
CIP
MN

Designed by Kathleen Lake

Manufactured in the United States of America.

Contents

New York, New York. Man, the place is crawling. Like the whole world was coming to town. One great big living room. Glass, stone, cash, noise, neon, fire sirens, potholes, sweltering summers. And plenty of jazz. Looking at Manhattan from the boat when you're coming in from the south of the island, you see something solid, lanky and proud. Narrow, muscular shoulders, lean-waisted, feet firmly planted. New York is no fatso, sprawling and bottom-heavy like L.A., or muscle-bound like Dallas. No, man—seen from street level, Manhattan's more like a long-distance runner, or maybe a pole vaulter. That's just the front, the outside, but when you step inside, it's like being backstage. It shakes, builds, tears down and eats up the past, and crashes headlong into the future. And it's hard to see how this place ever got the unlikely nickname "the Big Apple." An apple is something nice and sweet, with big round cheeks, its stem sticking out innocently. An apple comes from the sticks—it's modest and unsophisticated. But New York's just the opposite. The jazz musicians claim they came up with the nickname; because when you come there to play, you better be sure you're ready, or you'll feel a lump in your throat you can't swallow, a big Adam's apple.

Coming to town was something Thelonious Monk never had to do. He was a New Yorker almost from the start. The official biographies, after a few chronological backfires, finally trace his birth back to Rocky Mount, North Carolina, on October 10, 1917. While the Russian Revolution was exploding in the Old World, the United States was quietly celebrating its Black October—the birth of a jazz genius. And when he was four, his family packed up and moved to New York, where they settled in the midtown neighborhood of Manhattan known as San Juan Hill. Monk shared this privilege of living in the jazz capital of the world with a chosen few, such as Max Roach and Bud Powell. The other pioneers in the bebop adventure—the likes of Dizzy Gillespie, Miles Davis, Charlie Parker, Art Blakey, Oscar Pettiford, Kenny Clarke, and scores more, all had to make the trip to the Big Apple to prove themselves. Not Monk. He was right in the middle of it from the start.

If you played jazz and didn't live in New York, you always felt you were missing out on something. So when the bands of Duke Ellington or Fletcher Henderson came to your town, you dropped whatever you were doing and raced down to try and get in backstage. And if you had the nerve and were lucky enough, you got to jam later that night with some of the band. Then one of them might say, "You know, you don't play bad, kid. If you ever get to New York, give me a call." . . . Get to New York . . . See Harlem at last . . . because Harlem meant class . . . Harlem Rag, Harlem Stride, Harlem Hunch, Harlem—the one and only, with its masters and mistresses, its pastors and prophets of jazz.

Monk didn't have to move—he was already in Xanadu. You couldn't fool him—he knew. He grew up in the spot that later became Lincoln Center. Before, it was called San Juan Hill, his neighborhood was known as "the Jungle." 243 West 63rd Street. Right next door to the grand old jazz masters of New York, such as James P. Johnson, Willie "The Lion" Smith and Stephen "Beetle" Henderson. Picture Thelonious as a boy strolling around his neighborhood and hearing James P. through a window working out the chords on his piano of what would become his famous "Harlem Symphony." First-class sounds. The sounds of his own neighborhood. Two house fires, many world tours, international renown and all the money that goes along with it—none of it could make him leave his neighborhood, for there was the source of his energy and inspiration. Toward the end of his life, when the urge started to fade and he stopped playing, when he withdrew into himself and away from the world, he moved to the other shore—across the river that separates Manhattan from New Jersey.

The home of his friend, Baroness Pannonica de Koenigswarter, in Weehawken, New Jersey, has huge bay windows that give the visitor a splendid postcard view of the Manhattan skyline. When you've spent time in the bitter belly of the beast, and you stretch back and view it from afar, you start to sigh. Nothing can be stranger or more ambiguous than seeing New York from her living room. Born a Rothschild, and with a name like Pannonica, she was predestined to become the fairy godmother of the unrecognized geniuses of jazz. Being in her home is like stepping out of the struggle. And seeing the Manhattan skyline from her windows is certainly an aristocratic experience. Just cross the bridge, and you're back in the furnace. Then later, you return to the cool banks on the other side and reflect on what you've just seen or heard. You invite musicians to come and rehearse, play Ping-Pong, or just relax at Pannonica's. Lemonade in the summer, hot chocolate in the winter, always a bottle of good spirits in the cupboard and some grass to smoke—the Baroness's home, with its innumerable cats and its grand piano by the window, is a haven of luxury for social outcasts.

But Monk is ill, both physically and mentally. He came to live with his friend, the Baroness, not to recover, but to die.

Twenty-five years and twenty-eight days separate his first recording for Blue Note, and his final record appearance with the Giants of Jazz. His musical life had begun well before, and would continue long after, his last public appearance taking place in 1976 at the Newport Jazz Festival. But twenty-five years is a good round number. Twenty-five years that shook the world of music. Twenty-five years of visionary sounds, elliptical remarks, passion, and patience. Let's take a look.

‖ 1 ‖

Youth

Thelonious Monk grew up in the San Juan Hill section of Manhattan, with his mother Barbara Sphere Batts, his older sister Marion and his younger brother Thomas. His father, Thelonious Senior, returned to the South a few years after they had moved up north, following a serious illness, or so the story goes. He dropped out of sight completely until his death in a nearby Long Island hospital in 1969, unbeknownst to his son. Back then, San Juan Hill contained one of the largest black populations in New York, much bigger than that of Harlem, and remained a fashionable area up to the end of World War I. As might be expected, the several dozen blocks of houses were in sordid condition. More than twenty thousand blacks lived there, and the neighborhood was shaken by numerous violent revolts in 1905.

San Juan Hill was named after the Spanish-American War battle site which was valiantly taken by black soldiers of the American army in the struggle for Cuban independence. In memory of the efforts of these veterans, who now populated this section of Manhattan, President Theodore Roosevelt decided to launch a vast urban renewal project to provide standard, quality low-income housing in the area. The Monk family moved into a ground-floor apartment in one of the buildings. As the lucky recipient of one of the rare democratic gestures on the part of the New York real-estate promoters, Thelonious, from an early age, lived in an oasis of dignity, and modest but welcome comfort, which raised him above the poverty level of most of his fellow blacks. For a long time, this area of New York was a center of vital activity in the black civil-rights struggle and for the recognition of black culture as an integral part of American life.

Monk was gifted with a bright mind and was an exceptional student, particularly in math and physics (often the case among musicians). He became one of the very few black students to be accepted into the highly competitive Peter Stuyvesant High School. But he felt like something of an outsider. Of course, when your first name is Thelonious, like your father, and your middle name, Sphere, is your mother's middle name, and you have aunts and uncles on your father's side with names like Lorenzo and Squalillian, it's hard to go incognito.

The other kids must have given him a hard time in school. He stood out early, and long remained a popular figure around San Juan Hill. He was fascinated with fire trucks, and was adopted as mascot by the local firehouse. And his talent as a basketball player was recognized on all the local playgrounds. So, by all accounts, he was a boy who was perfectly adapted to life in the neighborhood. And it was there he soon encountered the loves of his life—first Ruby, his sister's best friend ("Ruby, My Dear"), and then Nellie, the girl who was to become his wife and lifelong companion.

He started off with the trumpet but dropped it immediately when the family purchased a player piano. The five-year-old was fascinated by the keys that moved by themselves. A player piano was also the best possible piano teacher, as you could hear the music while watching the keyboard play it at the speed you chose. As legend goes, that was how Art Tatum learned to play, adapting player-piano music written for four hands into music for two hands. This could also explain Thelonious's early taste for "stride" style, which was popular at the time, and available on player-piano rolls.

As in all respectable families, the big sister gets the piano lessons, and the little brother learns along with her. Later Monk told of how he learned to read music over his sister's shoulder, but at the age of eleven, he started taking private lessons from Marion's teacher, Mr. Wolff, and completed his apprenticeship with courses in harmony at the local conservatory. It was soon obvious that the boy only had to hear a tune once to be able to play it effortlessly on the piano. It is a well-known fact that some people are born with this gift, and Thelonious certainly was. He quickly put what he learned into practice by playing for neighborhood parties, and began practicing what he already knew would be his future profession. That was the secular side of Monk's music. For the sacred, as early as age nine, he spent his Sundays at the organ of St. Cyprien's Baptist Church accompanying his mother, who sang in the choir.

The only direct allusion Monk makes in his music to these Sundays in church is a brief, 53-second cut on

Monk's Music (Riverside, 1957), one of the most informative albums on his past. The cover shows Thelonious sitting with total nonchalance in one of those classic kiddy carts. Among the musicians featured on the recording is Coleman Hawkins, the first great jazz figure to have given Monk an opportunity, fourteen years earlier. This album could very well be seen as Monk's homage to his own past. And if I may take it even further, the little hymn, arranged for the piano in perfect counterpoint, is "Abide With Me" (which was also Fats Waller's favorite). Who wrote the hymn? None other than a nineteenth-century composer named—Monk.

Monk's playing of the organ pedals was a habit he picked up early, and this kind of foot movement became an integral and irreversible part of his body language, even when he was at the piano. You can almost hear another bass voice when you see Monk's feet making complicated figures on the floor while he is playing. For the piano has, at the most, only three very limited things called "expression pedals." What is that he's playing down there? An A-flat? A low G? Unfortunately, he was the only one who could hear it!

By the age of seventeen, with the concerned but confident support of his mother, he was determined to become a professional musician. He actually began with church music. For nearly two years he toured the States with a traveling female evangelist and gospel singer. The band that backed up the wandering preacher's sermons consisted of trumpet, saxophone, drums, and piano. As Monk himself said, with laconic humor, "Rock 'n' roll, or rhythm and blues. That's what we were doing. Only now they put different words to it. She preached and healed, and we played."

An unlikely beginning for the man who was to become

one of the chief instigators of the bebop revolution! Monk didn't have to dream about making the journey to New York, for he was already there. And he didn't set his sights on finding a place in the sun with some big band. Monk was neither pushy nor impatient.

This was certainly an essential episode in Monk's apprenticeship. And there is nothing surprising about the fact that he started his career in church. That is the well from which so many black American musicians first draw their musical inspiration. One could do a musical analysis of Monk's style, and its connection to the common core repertoire of church music. For example, the almost biblical simplicity of his voicings, which shift according to rules which are new yet familiar. And there is the constant adherence of these chords to the melody lines which so often dictate the harmony, as in the majority of hymns.

But to go off on tour with an evangelist for such a long time is rarer and of considerable importance. So much has been written on this type of music—classified, according to the instrumentation, as either "soul music," "gospel," or "Negro spirituals," and more easily referred to under the broader, more colloquial heading of "church music"—that little can be added. We Europeans hear something different in that expression: at worst "Nearer My God to Thee," or at best, Mozart's Requiem. However, for Monk, it was Baptist church music in particular he played, music of a much more intense and physical experience. This music calls for dance and movement. It is the very bond that joins the congregation together in their elevation toward God. It is the rhythm of mystical ecstasy.

For the jazz musician, playing this kind of music raises some interesting points, particularly: For whom is the music played? A simple question, but its answer entails an entire world of attitudes, aesthetics, and lifestyles. Inasmuch as the jazz player is an improviser, he sets himself apart from most other musicians of classical, pop, rock, or traditional forms who cling to "one" version of a composition, and play it the same way from one concert to the next. If they try to change something in the routine during a concert, the audience will make its displeasure known—they don't want anyone violating their certitudes.

Furthermore, the classical musician has to confront the delicate problem of interpretation, which brings up an infinite number of professional decisions of conscience. The rock musician confronts the problem of energy (the secrets of which range anywhere from diet to numerology, according to the depth of his convictions). But they are both freed from the obligation which requires the jazz musician, in each of his concerts, to attain improvisatory excellence, while maintaining the constant renewal of the means for reaching it. The challenge of improvising is to be ever new, and always good.

And then, usually, a musician will play music *for* someone else: the symphony member for the prima donna, the pop player for the lead singer, the dance band for the dancers. But jazz as it was played in Monk's time wasn't for any one group to the exclusion of others. First, it referred back to itself. The jazz musician plays for himself, for it is only within that world that he can find the necessary inventiveness for each moment. Second, he also plays for the other members of the band, because what he delivers takes them in one direction or another. And finally, he plays for the audience. Their attention is vital for him to reach the right degree of concentration, and their enthusiasm is the only true index of shared pleasure.

Some might say the problems are the same for the classical type of music known as chamber music. But in that case, the musician is, from the start, at the service of an ideal version which he must submit to and toward which he aspires. At home he practices a phrase twenty-five times to give it the proper dynamics, precision, and emotion. In jazz, there is no ideal version, and the performer does not know how the present version is going to turn out. Aside from a few basic conventions, nothing in a solo is prepared ahead of time. The player lets it roll, and sees what happens. The only references to cling to are yourself, the rest of the band, and perhaps the audience. And the major danger consists of closing yourself off from one of these references. The jazz musician who only plays for himself is isolated from the group, and becomes hermetic. The one who only plays for others will become dull and impersonal. And the musician who only plays for the audience—slowly but surely he will estrange himself from his art, because he will have sold his soul along the way.

When you are playing church music, these problems don't come up. The band is there to provide a musical illustration of one aspect or another of the sermon. But the most important function is that the music eventually *becomes* the sermon—the music embodies the faith and the spirit. The musician, the band, and the audience are no longer an issue. Everything is blended in a single emotion. Of course this type of music does not encourage daring improvisation; nevertheless it requires each musician to take an instinctive, improvised approach to the hymn being played. Each player has to find the most appropriate expression of this communal experience, while he is playing.

The essential part this music plays in the jazz musician's musical education is obvious. It awakens the sense of community which alone can prevent him from falling into the pitfalls of improvisatory music. It enables him to clarify from the beginning the vital question of whom he is playing for. It supports the ego, opens out onto the world, and awakens a person's sense of the mystical. By its very nature, it imposes that balance which is so difficult to find in jazz among hermeticism, convention and exhibitionism.

I can hear so much of the church in Thelonious's music. Not in the stylistic sense of a "churchy" chord, or a rhythm repeated *in the manner of*, as Horace Silver or Bobby Timmons does so well. Rather, in a much deeper, more radical sense: namely, Monk's way of solidifying a band with a single note, or of making it speak by a single rest. And then there are his melodies, both swinging and simple, repeated twenty times, like a mischievous hymn. This is not to be confused with the traditional sense of Milt Jackson's standard quotation, "Everybody wants to know where my style comes from, where I get it. Well, it comes from the church." Thelonious didn't get his *style* from the church, but rather the very *soul* of his music. By touring the States extensively with an evangelist, he witnessed the constantly renewed spectacle of the language of faith infused with music. Music that speaks. Music that makes people dance. Music that draws the ear to the regions where the soul is elevated, wilder, and, too, more serene. That is the music of Thelonious. An unshakable faith in himself, in his work, and in a power that guides him, shines forth each time he sits down at the piano. He has a strange and characteristic magnetism, and a way of getting attention with just one note.

To me, this reveals a mystical belief in his art which he acquired quite young. According to all accounts, this belief emerged full-blown when he was only an adolescent.

And Monk had religion on all sides. First of all from his mother Barbara, who became a Jehovah's Witness in the 1940's. His younger brother Thomas toyed with the idea of boxing professionally, and then put on the NYPD blue uniform, but he left the police for fear of having to kill one of his own. Converted by his mother, he too became a Jehovah's Witness. So, on the one hand, from his mother and brother there was the unquestioning faith in the sacred texts, and on the other, his father's mysterious illness, a carefully-kept family secret which caused him to disappear completely from the family horizon. Sadly, even today, fathers' disappearances from black families of modest circumstances is common. Unfortunately, the scenario is often much simpler—Dad's in jail, or else he went out for a stroll, and never came back. In the case of the Monk family, where moral strength and a belief in one's dignity were taken for granted, the father's absence remained a question mark. And the children could guess, by the embarrassed silence of the aunts and uncles, that the mystery of that absence would weigh heavily on their destinies.

‖ 2 ‖

Minton's

onk left adolescence and approached adulthood as a jack-of-all-trades piano player. He is said to have accompanied singer Helen Humes for two years (1936–37), in Albany, New York, where Prohibition, and the presence of a corrupt mayor, had paradoxically encouraged people to indulge themselves, and, in so doing, to listen to jazz. At that time, Thelonious must have seen his share of the wild side. He would have learned what it meant to be a black youth in a violent and racist urban context. He surely saw the police working hand in glove with the gangsters they were supposed to be prosecuting. Friends of his being beaten up because they opened their mouths at the wrong time. Thousands of dollars changing hands right in front of him while he got small change for a night's work. This was all part of the required apprenticeship if you were to make it through your twenties without getting in too much trouble.

And in 1939 he turned up as piano player in a Chinese restaurant next to the Savoy Ballroom in Harlem. According to Mary Lou Williams who heard him in Kansas City when he came through there with the evangelist, Thelonious—who was only eighteen at the time—already had a style all his own. He was not even twenty, but was already determined to follow his own path and find a sound of his own. But the originality of his playing style—he made no concessions—never prevented him from "playing the gig." Monk never talked much, but many years later, he briefly mentioned this period: "A lot of things in life are hard to remember . . . but you always remember the bad stuff." But by the time he landed at Minton's in the late 1930s, he was experienced. Monk had been around.

Minton's Playhouse was a Harlem jazz club located at 210 West 118th Street, between Seventh and Eighth Avenues, a few blocks from the mythical Apollo Theater, where so many black artists began their careers. Thelonious won first prize at the famous Wednesday amateur night so often that he was eventually barred from entering it. With his usual good sense, years later Monk confided that this rebuff convinced him it was time to turn professional. Minton's had the usual jazz-club format, with a concert in several sets each night, interspersed with various other acts. But Henry Minton had two great ideas which made his club a favorite with Harlem jazz musicians. The first was to provide a free dinner (and the food was said to be excellent) each week to any musician who was playing at the Apollo down the street. Every Monday, on their day off, the cream of the jazzmen would come by—from the bands of Duke Ellington, Count Basie, Cab Calloway, and so many others. Little by little, many of them got in the habit of stopping by on other nights after their shows, thus adding to the little club's prestige.

The other great idea was to organize an official jam session after the house band had played its sets. This was a very clever commercial move—the musicians who came by to jam started off eating for free, but then wound up playing for free. The proximity of the Apollo naturally made these first-class sessions. Saxophonist and renowned band leader Teddy Hill was master of cere- monies, and he chose Kenny Clarke to lead the house band. Kenny brought in Joe Guy on trumpet, bassist Nick Fenton and, on piano, Thelonious Monk.

For a jazz musician's development, playing in a club is vital: when playing music which is so dependent on im- provisation, it's essential to sharpen your reflexes, your ear, and your mind on the spot. In other words, there are many things you can only learn on the bandstand. At home, you can practice a phrase, a tune, or a chord as much as you want. But when you're on the bandstand, any number of outside factors can affect your carefully prepared work. The band might choose to play it in a different key or tempo than the one you've practiced. Maybe the house piano is out of tune in one octave and you have to find another spot on the keyboard to play the same idea. Maybe the trumpet player has indigestion from wolfing down a hasty dinner and skips a line in the opening bars. The drummer might be distracted for a moment by some girl's smile and turns the beat around. And that means trouble. Or the bass is too soft, and the quality and pitch of the accompaniment is compromised. The list is endless.

So, when you are a young musician with sharp, new ideas about jazz, you must find a club where you can play on a regular basis with the same band, a place which will serve as a kind of laboratory for your ideas. Practice makes perfect, as the saying goes. That's why the jazz clubs play such an important part in the development of this music. And that's why I'd rather, when I can, go and hear a jazz band in a club rather than in a concert hall where some of that essential spontaneity can be lost.

But what were the oppportunities for jazz musicians to play in 1940? There were hotel ballrooms and dance halls which usually had big bands. These were great, but the music was written out and highly arranged. There were radio broadcasts, usually direct from these halls, or from the studios. This had its constraints, too, as you had to give the listeners shorter versions, with abridged solos. A good exercise, maybe, but not quite the real thing. And then there was the club. It is ideal for letting go, and trying out new material. And even if it doesn't work, what counts is to just jump right in! And then, when the player is not afraid or holding back, he starts playing better and coming up with ideas like never before.

So there was Monk at Minton's. The club was like a magnet for whomever was playing in New York, but it would be a mistake to think that, at that time, the club was offering a completely modern and abstruse music which broke with contemporary standards. That was far from the case. But the players were looking, hunting, and experimenting without knowing where it was all leading. A trumpet player like Joe Guy, for example, wasn't revolutionary. Hot Lips Page or Herbie Fields, who were among Minton's regulars, weren't modernists and didn't consider themselves as such.

One of the only indisputable innovators in that inner circle of club musicians, aside from Clarke or Monk, was the guitarist Charlie Christian. He had mastered and embelished a new and very simple technical idea: the amplified, or electric, guitar. The new instrument allowed him to step out of the standard rhythmic accompaniment for which he was known and to start phrasing his solos like a trumpet or a saxophone. As soon as he hit New York, Benny Goodman invited him to join the band. The problem was that Goodman, the clarinetist, even though he hired certain members of the black musical elite of the day, was primarily using them for his advantage, leaning on them to highlight his own talent as an instumentalist and improviser.

The hierarchy was obvious and, though it was one of the best-paid jobs around, no musician could ever get in Benny's way. As a result, as soon as one of Benny's concerts ended, Christian headed straight for Minton's where he could play as many solos as he liked without having to worry about upstaging anyone.

The Harlem sessions served a crucial purpose: when a musician finished his work, he could enjoy himself without worrying about losing his gig. It should not be forgotten that these were young musicians, who were trying to earn a living in the touring bands, the leaders of which were more preoccupied with making ends meet than with musical innovation. But Monk's position was special as his gig at Minton's earned him his livelihood, and was not just an outlet for letting off steam after the constraints of conventional bands. So, with the Kenny Clarke quartet, he was at the very heart of this laboratory of musical research. And, contrary to all the visiting guests from other bands who stepped up to the stand, Monk had to give his work all the seriousness and concentration required of a steady musical job.

A few recordings of these nights at Minton's survive. A young student at Columbia University named Jerry Newman was lucky enough to own a device for recording and playing records, which he used in the club for a mime act. His performances to recordings of celebrities like Roosevelt or Churchill were definitely crowd-pleasers. But Jerry was well aware of the quality of the music being played around him. He took advantage of the situation and recorded a number of nights at Minton's (as well as in other clubs), recordings which now still surface regularly on pirate labels throughout the world (claiming that it's Monk you can hear behind Charlie Christian, although, unfortunately, they were never recorded together). According to those who were there at the time, these records do not do justice to Monk's "troubling" modernism. But it is possible to gain some idea of what was going on at Minton's during the developing years of the young pianist.

What strikes me first is the pulse of these recordings. In the early 1940s, the killer grooves in New York came from Kansas City, and the killer soloists came from Kansas City, too: Ben Webster, Lester Young, Jo Jones, soon Charlie Parker, and especially Count Basie. Basie's rhythm section was the finest in any swing band anywhere. It swung, it rocked, it grooved. They played "clock time," and it made you want to jump like the sweep second-hand. It was the "in" thing, and everybody wanted more. This rhythmic idea served as a basis for soloists of all styles, young or old, classic or modern.

They all fitted in and the red carpet seemed to roll out by the hour, inviting everyone in to the kind of music that never wanted to stop.

Like all the others, Monk adopted this approach, and on the records he plays the piano accordingly, "in the old style," as he often later did in solo. This meant playing the "pump" with the left hand, in the pure stride tradition (a bass note alternating every other beat with a chord), for maximum swing. But the advantage of this technique, if you have an open-enough mind, is that the right hand is free to do whatever it wants. Monk plunged into this opening and built up and over his left hand, creating colors, rhythms, and figures with a right hand as free as the breeze.

The left hand was classic, and the right was modern. Take away the left hand and there would be the Monk of twenty years later. Remove the right, and it would be back to the jazz of twenty years earlier. The last time I heard somebody using a similar technique, it was Don Pullen, shortly before he died. On a standard type of composition, with a repetitive rhythmic figure, he beat out the regular pulse of the tune with his left hand, and improvised compeletely "free" with his right hand. The effect was unforgettable: comfort and surprise combined; sweet and sour; the sun alongside the moon. But, it wasn't the stylistic or technical performance that was so immediately captivating. It wasn't mere flourish. On the contrary, it was magical and that combination released unsuspected dynamic powers. But it's all hell to control! Better not play at sorcerer's apprentice with magic like that or you'll be in deep trouble quick. It's like voodoo; so watch your step! This early technique is, I think, one of the reasons why Monk later charmed so many of the big family of free-jazz players. From his early days, he had found a way to get new lava to flow—good and red and telluric. His was a new energy; a machine for making brand-new sounds. And it was there, at Minton's, that the new recipe was simmering.

One man stood out in the midst of these innovators. He embodied the voice of the times: John Birks "Dizzy" Gillespie. He is the one who theorized, staked the claim and who brought the scattered troops together. He was the ambassador of the "new ideas," the man who spoke. He was usually the link with the press, as he wasn't camerashy. And for a journalist, someone who can talk is precious, especially when he says things that are new, interesting, and disturbing. Then, good articles get written and people come out to hear the new music.

This army of new musicians had an agenda, as well. It may have owed nothing to Lenin, but it was definitely political. With the jazz of the 1940s, quickly labeled "bebop," there appeared a new deal in the New York social contract: blacks were beginning to speak out and to defend certain positions. America was at war, and in order to send men to the front, some of the pressure at home had to be relaxed. Under the aegis of their mouthpiece Dizzy, whose verve as an orator was equaled only by his instrumental dexterity, a mass of black individuals gathered who reflected growing discontent. Of all the great jazzmen of the day, however, Monk and Parker would be the only ones—officially—not to join in the outspoken protest. They shared a profound certitude: their art spoke so much louder than words. But whether it was Max Roach, the most intellectual of them all, or Art Blakey, Oscar Pettiford or Kenny Clarke, one way or another they all spoke out against the unbearable official racism that existed at the time.

But to return to the birth of this new music, it is well known that the majority of bebop tunes are based on a paraphrase of compositions that already existed. By using the harmonic lines of the hit tunes of the day, the boppers did not really compose, as much as they pirated. In response to the flourishing "variety music" industry whose success was indebted to black music, and whose profits wound up in the white man's pocket, Dizzy and his followers figured they were only getting their own back. For example, none of Charlie Parker's compositions, except for perhaps *Confirmation*, was based on an original chord progression. This is not the case with Monk, but we'll come back to that later. The overarching system of Bird and Diz's chord substitutions enriched the original material and supported all kinds of musical diversity, the fluid strangeness of which exploded the conventions of improvisation.

The titles themselves of these new tunes seemed to celebrate the advent of a new spirit in this music which America (and Europe of the time) would only accept in its danceable, hedonistic, and most basic form. "Honeysuckle Rose" or "On the Sunny Side of the Street" would be replaced by "Evidence" or "Now's the Time." I always loved Bird's cynical irony in naming "Relaxin' at Camarillo," the blues he wrote while he was a patient at the California psychiatric hospital of the same name.

But whether iconoclastic or innovative, this new jazz called bebop became, at the time, an affair of the intellectuals. Up to then, the appeal of jazz had been its immediacy and body language. Now, ideas were becoming part of the music as well. As a matter of fact, some tempos were too hard to dance to, and only the mind can encompass them to the exclusion of the body. In his autobiography, Dizzy Gillespie insists on the intellectual and musical authority he as a trumpet player acquired by being familiar with the piano, the most intellectual of all instruments. Throughout his life he taught the mysteries of that orchestra of black and white keys to whomever would listen. The generation of melodists would be replaced by the proud and exclusive club of harmonists.

And nothing was spared to keep this club exclusive. To protect themselves from the older musicians who were always ready to give lessons in the course of the jam sessions, the boppers took refuge behind the speed-of-light tempos, which filtered out undesirables and sent them back to practice their instruments. And the vast complex range of flatted ninths, fifths, and thirteenths, passing and substitute chords, made the terrain even more treacherous for the uninitiated musician.

And here Monk stepped in as "High Priest of Bebop," as he was so elegantly baptised when, around 1946, this music acquired a name, a body of tunes, leadership, and articles in the newspapers. Of all his contemporaries, his ideas were the strongest. And to play Monk's music, one had to think. It is no accident that he was, along with Kenny Clarke, the author of an early bopper anthem: when they wanted to get rid of somebody, they went into the amazing "Epistrophy." The tempo was not impossible and a lot of tunes at the time were played much faster. But it contained all the idiosyncrasies of that new school of playing, from its melody with strange intervals to its harmonic structure based on half-steps. This was not a rhythmic repellent, but a *harmonic* one. Watch your head, not your step!

At the time, America considered this invasion of new ideas into music as nothing short of impudence. Not that the mind had been banished from jazz before bop—the great genius Duke Ellington had been making his mark for years. And, to mention only one other, Art Tatum had been thrilling the most eminent musicologists, including pianist Vladimir Horowitz. But these were individuals, and not schools. They were accepted, tolerated, assimilated, and even respected on their own. The boppers, on the other hand, were a tight-knit group held together by a compact and incendiary agenda. And Monk, with his strange silences, enigmatic smiles, and his general attitude reminiscent of what Dashiell Hammett referred to as "the other side of a half-wit," embodied irony and protest more than anyone else. Dizzy always expressed his positions on subjects concerning black life with verve and brio. He could combine a highly developed sense of his own affairs with an outspoken criticism of a cruel and racist society. He was able to strike the fine line which enabled him to be both a musician of genius *and* an entertainer, without becoming a buffoon. His exuberance had charm, but never made him appear ridiculous. Monk, too, had a head full of exuberance, with his wild hats, his glasses, and his savory comments. But Monk wasn't a charmer. He only sought to charm himself.

So the first voice you heard belonged to Diz. Everything about him recalled the spoken word, the magical chant. His cheeks swelled out amazingly when he put the trumpet to his lips. His entire appearance changed when he expressed himself with his horn. And, a few years later, when he twisted the bell of his trumpet up, he made his desire to speak even more visible. When he was playing in the Cab Calloway band, he sang, "I'm Diz the Whiz, a swinging hip cat, Diz the Whiz!" He was already "rapping"; the forefather of acid jazz— Dizzy could talk the talk.

And he was also the link between Parker and Monk.

For, not far from Minton's, at a place called Monroe's, the same thing was going on. The Monroe brothers, Clark and Jimmy, had opened a club like Minton's which had the particularity of "opening" at 4:01 A.M. As clubs, by law, had to close at four A.M. they ingeniously managed to create an "after-hours" place that jazzmen of all styles flocked to when they'd finished playing their gigs, or jamming at Minton's. The word was out: "Let's make it to Monroe's Uptown House—Bird's playing with Diz, and we can sit in!" Of course, nobody got much sleep back then. The music began at dusk and went on up till noon the next day. So it's not surprising that the music made a huge leap forward in only a few years. On the other hand, many musicians died far too young, for when you add drugs to the scene, it's not really what you'd call a healthy lifestyle.

Gillespie shuttled between the two clubs, a set at one, a jam at the other, like a jazz ambassador. And after the war, when things started to settle down, people could see that the boppers were well on their way to creating something totally new. But here again, something exceptional was happening. Logically, Monk should have followed the movement, and wound up in 1947 playing like everybody else. However, he had been composing. And in '47, when he cut his first record for Blue Note, that company had about as much to do with bebop as Louis-Ferdinand Céline did with the Surrealists. André Breton and Céline were only two years apart, but what a difference! On one side, a charismatic individual who started a whole school and network; and on the other, a totally solitary and independent artist. As music critic Paul Bacon says, "The major difficulty with Monk's first recordings was in finding young musicians who *could* play his music." While all the others were swept up into the exalting constellations of

Bird and Diz, Monk dug in and cut his own path. In 1946, Diz hired him for his band, but it didn't last long, and Monk was soon replaced by John Lewis.

And yet . . . it is impossible to imagine bop without Monk. He was there when it all began, and yet it's as if, at a certain moment, he decided to say, Later fellas; you can go on without me—I got another scene to make. Undoubtedly, this had been his attitude from the beginning, but as time passed, it became clearer: Monk was on his own. Still, his door was always open to other musicians, and he'd go round from one jam session to the next all night long. He wasn't sitting alone in his corner, just mulling over his tunes; on the contrary, he was at the heart of the action. He was the spiritual big brother of the man who came to be known as the *real* bop piano player, Bud Powell. Everyone in Harlem knew who Thelonious Monk was, and his name was uttered with respect. But just like the character in Rudyard Kipling's *Just-So Stories*, he was The Cat That Walked by Himself.

And the big question that musicologists and jazz historians have always been asking about this period is, Who got what from whom? Was it Diz who taught the flatted minor fifth chords to Bird? And did he steal Monk's material? Was Max Roach influenced by Blakey? Did Bud push the music further than Bird, and was Bird jealous of him? Concerning this period in the history of jazz, the question of genealogy is inevitable. As if the local hobby club was awarding a prize for the "inventor of bebop." What's the point? There's always someone else. When speaking of Charlie Christian, Dizzy says he was nothing compared to John Collins, who was much more harmonically advanced. And there was no better judge than Diz. But then you could also ask John Collins who gave him the spark to start playing like he did. And so on. Jazz, like all the other arts, has always encouraged healthy competition. This cat's better than that one; so-and-so's better, et cetera. So what? Because in the end, you wind up listening to them all, and that's what counts. The sad thing is when you begin to choose just one, for that's the beginning of dogmatism and the end of art.

Be that as it may, Monk was writing away in his corner. And, from the moment he was admitted into the select circle of hip Harlem musicians, he was recognized as an unparalleled composer. The other musicians spent their time working on improvisation techniques— on playing the complex harmonies that were substituted for the ones you usually heard, with speed and dexterity. Not Monk. In fact, he developed his improvisation according to the chosen tune and tempo. He wouldn't play the same type of phrase for a ballad as he would for an up-tempo tune. The boppers, on the other hand, would practice a phrase slowly, then faster and faster, until they worked their way up to the desired tempo. A funny thing happens, then, in the "up-tempo" tunes, for you are listening to music that's going too fast for your ears. The boppers' dexterity consisted of stringing phrases together in a steady cadence—phrases that are all gems of musical intelligence that can only be appreciated a few seconds after you've heard them. It is a sort of cascading ecstasy. Like a necklace of rare pearls, strung together one by one at top speed. Which led Thelonious to say, in a memorable interview in *Downbeat* magazine, when he was listening to an Art Pepper record, "It sounded like some slow solos speeded up, to me." This is an essential point, for it once again brings up the question of improvisation in general, and its relation to the specific tempo and harmonies of each tune.

Word was getting around: Thelonious was raising a lot of questions. Well, not verbal ones, as he wasn't exactly talkative, but by his highly personal music, so different from all the trends. As he later said himself, all he wanted to do was to write nice songs. So it is just as hard to associate him with the first wave of boppers, as it is to disassociate him, because they're the ones he raised the questions for. For all the young musicians who were so anxious to make use of new tunes and new harmonies, he was the first, and just about the only one offering something new and unique. It may be hard to imagine now, but a tune like "Round Midnight" was unbelievably difficult for an improviser back then. Not from a technical point of view, but because of the effort required just to get it to sound right. Miles Davis confessed that it took him years to be able to play it the way he wanted. Monk swamped his contemporaries with atypical tunes, forcing the improviser to sit down and say to himself, Okay, hold on; let's see how this thing works. Whereas the other tunes of nascent bebop seem to favor reflexes, symmetries, and ready-made progressions, most of Monk's tunes are like a roadblock barring the way to routine, systematic improvisation. And it is not difficulty for its own sake—far from it. As soon as you hear the tunes, you want to play them . . . and that's where the trouble starts.

The boppers soon invaded 52nd Street. In the 1930s, there were the "uptown" clubs of Harlem which had become an essential center of black culture, and the "downtown" clubs of 52nd Street. This was the standard split in the jazz world between "black" clubs and "white" clubs. In short, downtown was the showcase of jazz for tourists, artificially condensed into a single street where sailors, celebrators, connoisseurs, curiosity seekers, or journalists could take their ears for a treat. This was the Disney World of jazz. Street hawkers, flashing neon signs, and the upper crust out slumming. But uptown, you had the real stuff. Up there, the average listener knew what was going on, and was familiar with the musicians, the bands, the various influences and the history of jazz. Harlem adopted the boppers long before they went down to 52nd Street, and that's why they are still talking about Minton's, Monroe's, the Apollo, or the Savoy Ballroom. When you're black, uptown is the place you go to school. You go down to 52nd Street for the money, to get seen by the journalists, get heard by the big wheels, the agents and the record companies. Harlem wasn't off-limits to white musicians; there were just very few of them who were open to the new music known as bop. And as the general trend in Harlem was to reject that white culture which had for so long monopolized the business and commercial aspects of jazz; if you wanted to make it, you really had to dig in. In closing, it should be added that segregation, still in effect in New York in the 1940s, was, according to Max Roach, a damn good thing: in Harlem it encouraged a sort of caste mentality—like a hothouse in which black culture could bloom freely. In Harlem, you played. On 52nd Street, you earned your living by playing.

But earning a living was never a major preoccupation for Thelonious, who didn't join the others in their invasion of that famous Swing Street. Of course you would see him at the Spotlite alongside Coleman Hawkins (with whom he would make his first recording a year later); or with Kenny Clarke at Kelly's Stable, or even at the Onyx Club in August of '43 with the Dizzy Gillespie band. But never with a band under his own name. He was too young, too introverted, and his music was too difficult. He wasn't playing the game. He already had his own voice and he was perfecting a style in which he was developing not only an extremely modern idea of harmony, but also nothing less than a new approach to rhythm.

‖ 3 ‖

Rhythm Section

When you're strolling down a hillside street on a summer night after a few drinks, you just feel like singing. It's almost automatic: momentarily released from the pull of gravity, walking is effortless, worries fade, and you start to sing—whatever comes to mind: opera if the street is resonant, jazz if it's dark, or the Beatles if you're really drunk. Having had their sleep disturbed so often, people who live on a hillside street are well aware of this phenomenon.

That feeling of rich and natural weightlessness, where life is simple and all sounds are in tune is, I believe, the closest thing to the feeling you get from a good rhythm section. When the rhythm section is bad, it's like a hill you have to climb, carrying a big package under your arm, being careful not to slip on the rain-soaked cobblestones. A passable rhythm section is like a long flat road bordered by orderly rows of plain trees—you keep on walking, striding regularly, straight ahead to your destination.

When Monk began his career as a piano player, jazz was in the midst of inventing a new instrumental color: the close combination of the bass, drums, and piano. That's what you saw in all the bebop bands. Since then, it's become such a standard format that it's difficult to imagine that anything else ever existed. Yet in the early 1940s, it was brand-new. But what about Basie? one might say. Well, he had a guitar player, and not just *any* guitar player, but Freddie Green, the human metronome. In fact, piano, bass, guitar, and drum combos were everywhere in the late 1930s. Some groups even dropped the drums, like Nat King Cole or Clarence Profit, but not having a guitar was unthinkable. Its rhythmic and harmonic contribution, which blended marvelously with both the piano syncopation and the bass lines, was too precious to be abandoned. And yet . . .

Twenty years earlier, even the bass was rarely used. But this critical instrument had been developing rapidly, and by the 1940s had received its pedigree thanks to musicians like Jimmy Blanton and Milt Hinton. No longer content just to relieve the left hand of the piano player, who did not have to play the roots of the chords, the bass became a solo instrument, and joined the grand family of improvising instruments. The drums, freed by Kenny Clarke from having to play all four beats on the bass drum, could now take off into more and more complex rhythmic patterns. As for the piano, it continued its harmonic evolution which progressively drew it away from the guitar. Ask a guitarist to play a Monk tune as faithfully as possible and you will see him frown and grimace. It's all happening too fast for that stringed instrument. In fact, the guitar was acquiring the status of a hybrid, for it encroached on the imperialistic development of the bass, piano and drums. The days of the guitar at the heart of the rhythm section were numbered, and when Monk came on the scene, pianists had to invent a new sound—that of the trio.

It all started with the bass and drums. It's often thought that a good bass player and a good drummer will make a good pair—like a right and a left shoe. But an Italian loafer and an English riding boot don't go together, even if they are the same size. You'll soon have blisters, and won't get very far. The moral of the story? Find the right pair.

In a lighter vein, there's nothing funnier or more moving than the shotgun marriage of the bass and drums, the two heaviest portable instruments in the band, excluding the piano. On tour, bassists and drummers begin to think *heavy*, it's a whole way of life, an entire philosophy. Special tickets, extra seats, wider stairways and doors, and proper temperatures are all required. (The double bass can open up like an old shoe if it's too hot or humid, or can split like a log if it's too cold.) They're stablemates from the Ranch of the Heavyweights. And, to make matters worse, bassists and drummers never travel light. Besides their instruments, they always have bags full of tools, gadgets, medicine, who knows what— like women's handbags, there is always a surprise inside. Once they're onstage, plugged in and grounded, with their stuff spread all around (with an authority that can only come from weight and size), you'd better not to mess with them. They've come to work, and it's hard enough as it is.

And that's when the miracle takes place. The lights dim, the house goes quiet, and there's one instant when nothing has happened yet. A moment later it will be too late, for the clock is wound tight and time will start ticking, but here, for the moment, there's nothing, simply the promise, or the threat, of time. Then, suddenly, everything changes, and the bass and drums, with furious joy, lay out the route which each instant leads us closer to our death.

Once they're onstage, the responsibility of these two heavyweights is enormous, and that's why they need so many spare parts—for they have to create nothing less than time itself. This is a far cry from the sadistic and fastidious expression of *keeping the beat*. No—they *make time*. Not the ticking of the second hand on the watch face; rather, a deep pulse which has always throbbed in the marrow of our bones, and which helps us to forget the other Time.

In the course of the concert, the Pair become the Masters of Time! And that is no simple matter. Why does it always take at least two people to make time? Surely it's because when you're alone, it is your word against the rest of the world, and that is the beginning of fanaticsm. When you are two together, it's the beginning of a shared experience, a faith expressing itself, faith in a god which is the original pulse, and which is worshiped in a church that is the music itself. Creating time is a truly mystical and communal experience. What we blindly seek alone, with disarming fragility (you sneeze—poof!—you lost the beat), when you're together, you find it with exhilarating facility. It's an act of love, as opposed to masturbation.

I've always believed that rhythms existed before man, and that they floated around virtually within each of us. Those who create time are merely placing themselves in unison with that primordial frequency—like putting your fingers into an electrical outlet, then not being able to pull them away. For the pulse is there all around us. Our life span is a voyage down a river of rhythm. We are born into it, and we die upon it. How powerful and wise is the person who knows how to channel and transmit that force! Glory be to those who awaken us to that rhythm which speaks within us. All God's children got rhythm!

When you see a protozoa through a microscope, it looks like it's dancing to a James Brown record played at 78 rpm. And in science class I couldn't help imagining tiny cymbals or drums at the ends of the parameciums' vibrating hairs, as they made microscopic music. What a band! You wouldn't be able to hear yourself think. And just how is mankind conceived? To the rhythms of the mattress springs! Life itself means rhythm. From the regular contractions of the mother's womb as it releases the fetus, to the infant's first experiences of sleep and feeding, everything happens in rhythm. Small or large; short rhythms that last a split second, or long ones that last ten years; ones that crisscross or echo each other, ones that prevent you from spinning your wheels, or others that inflate you like a ball. You can't choose these kinds of rhythms any more than you can choose the day you're born, because you can't be one beat ahead of the rhythm. Yes, indeed! Glory to those ingenious handymen who can organize this rhythm, spin it around, wind it up, capture and tame it, and put it in their little music box, like the first men once did with fire!

That's how important the bass and drums are! Bring on the crown, the purple robe, the incense and precious stones! Show them the respect they deserve; the fear and awe, in fact. Any ill will or reluctance on their part and the whole night of music is ruined. With a sad saxophone player, or an out-of-tune piano, you can wing it. It's a little off but that won't spoil the show. But if the bass player and the drummer don't do their job, everything falls apart! You don't pay attention to the two heavyweights because they're playing all the time. You get used to them, like they're part of the furniture. Now and then, the rest of the band stops and you're surprised to discover that maybe the bass does have a soul, and that the drummer can play with finesse. But if one of them just happens to stop playing, the band goes into free fall! There is no way out; no rip cord to pull! It is easy to see how nervous the band gets when the bass player is late for the gig—without him, you have to cancel! The trumpet player may have lost his front teeth, or the pianist the use of his right hand, the show must go on, even without them. But without a bass player, forget it. They know it, too, and you can't hold it against them; It would be like reproaching the sun for coming up in the morning—that's just the way it is. They hold in their hands the absolute power of *gravity*. There is no one beneath the bass player, so he *must* be right. If he plays a wrong note, it sounds like the piano player is off. These are the laws of the human ear: you hear sounds from bass to treble, so you better get used to it. The bass player is always right, and that's all there is to it.

Same thing for the drummer: along with the bass, he's the one who establishes and amplifies the time. The bass sketches out time with a primordial pulsation, and the drums draw it in India ink. The crystalline precision of the ride cymbal. The shrewd and solid comments of the snare and bass drums. Depth, contour, innuendo, doors that open and close as the drumskin is struck. And if the drummer decides to play "Summertime" as a tango, you can always curse him out afterward, but there in concert, you just have to go along with him. It's the opposite of the lemming phenomenon—when you *don't* follow the drummer, that's when you're in trouble. The bass and the drums are the instruments which keep us in contact with the ancient beauty of rhythm. The gut string you pluck, and the stretched skin you strike—what could be more carnal, more animal, than that?

Take a goat: strings can be made from the guts, drums from skin, the bones make decent drumsticks, and you can eat the rest. A whole band on four hooves, and nothing is wasted. How many movable parts are there on a piano? And how many bends between the mouthpiece and the bell of a trumpet? And how do all those keys on a saxophone work? It's hard to say! But a child of three can understand how a bass or a drum works. You pluck, you pull, you strike, and the music starts. This old couple, the guts and the skin, have been around for so long, since the dawn of time in fact, that we tend to take them for granted. But with the advent of bebop, they were sudddenly out there on their own. Gone were the warm chords of the guitar to light the way for the bass player and lighten the load for the drummer.

These two heavyweights have to get along well together. If they play one against the other, it just doesn't work. They must play one *within* the other in order for the music to be at its best, and that doesn't always happen. It's a Zen experience. One creates the red, the other creates the yellow, and together they produce a magnificent and sacred shade of orange. Color gradation is forbidden, as are half-shades, yellowish streaks, and sloppy drippings. A good rhythm section is a fine pure shade of orange, smooth and even. It should never skid. Time is a river and the drummer and bass player control its flow right down to the smallest drop. One on either bank of the river, they are the ferrymen of time.

And then there's the piano. A relatively recent arrival to music, it's an engineer's nightmare of complexity. A whole orchestra at your fingertips. Percussive, melodic, and harmonic, it's the king of the jungle. This diabolical invention enables you to do away with all the other instruments. It absorbs them and, like the intellectual of the family, tells them what to do and bosses them around. And what a piece of furniture: hammers, pedals, dampers, wood, cast iron, leather, steel, springs, felt, screws, and ivory. True bulk. This is the only instrument which the musician doesn't tune himself. The piano provides a livelihood for furniture movers, tuners, and pianists. It feeds a whole family by itself. A noble instrument: complicated, generous, and imposing.

It took awhile for the piano to join up with the bass and drums. It began as somewhat of an outsider owing to its classical background. When a steady, dancing rhythm and harmony had to be expressed, a technique was used which had been developed by pianists of the Romantic period, and which later became known as "stride." But by Monk's time, it had all changed. A new jazz sound was emerging. First of all with Basie, who simplified rhythm down to its quintessence and placed the piano upon a thick, luxurious carpet of sound. He proved once and for all that you could swing more with fewer notes, by letting the bass, drums, and guitar do the work. Then the boppers required the piano to perform, which propelled the music to new heights.

The modern pianist has a very special relationship with his drummer and his bassist. As his instrument has hammers, it resembles the drums; and as it has strings, it's like the bass. His position in the rhythm section is more detached, and more ambiguous than that of his partners, the bass and the drums. If he feels like it, he can stop playing for a few bars and let the bass define the harmony and the drums ensure the rhythm. He can suggest new harmonic directions, fall into step with a soloist, then break away a moment later. On again, off again. He opens or he closes. He's present at the heart of the rhythm, then suddenly he's gone. Nothing like the two others who continuously express the rhythmic pulse with their arms and legs. The pianist doesn't have the possibility of letting his body speak in order to express time. Just watch his feet—the only place where time physically flows. As for the hands, with ten square inches of skin, he can stir up an object that weighs a thousand pounds.

That's where Monk comes in. For he can do what very few piano players are capable of: when he plays, he is a full rhythm section all by himself. He invents a piano method which enables us to hear a continuous tempo beneath all the unpredictable flights of his piano virtuosity. He's three-in-one. Many years later, his son recalled how he began his career as a jazz drummer in his father's band. He said it was like floating on a magic carpet. Dad set up the tempo, he said, and you were carried along by his playing. It was only when he left his father's band and found himself in less exceptional circumstances that he realized that a band expects the drums, and not the piano, to keep the beat.

To accomplish this, Thelonious perfected an original technique. Seeing him at the piano, you understand this quickly: he makes no wasted movement, and his touch is amazingly diverse and dynamic. One note is barely caressed, while another is pounded or crushed. How can he be so upredictable and precise at the same time? It seems impossible on the piano.

In fact, Monk doesn't physically play like a piano player. He plays more like a vibraphonist. A pianist sits perpendicular to the instrument, with his arms moving sideways and his hands curved over the keys in order to attain maximum speed of phrasing by enabling the thumb to pass under the fingers. The pianist seldom looks at the keyboard. The vibraphonist leans over the instrument, constantly crossing his arms for obvious technical reasons (he only uses two mallets, or, at most, four). Thus, he uses all his weight to accent one note or another, which he chooses for its rhythmic or melodic quality. The mallets are held straight out, parallel to the metal, bladelike keys of the instrument. If you watch Monk play (if only for that, the excellent movie by Charlotte Zwerin, *Straight, No Chaser*, is available on videocassette), you'll be struck by the fact that he seems to dominate the keyboard with all his weight, as opposed to someone like Bill Evans or Glenn Gould, who keep their foreheads practically glued to the keys.

I have to admit that seeing Monk play was a revelation for me. After innumerable attempts to transcribe some of his tunes or his characteristic lines, I was unable to capture the soul of his music, simply because I was missing the *sound*. Also, I couldn't seem to accent some of his phrases the way he did it. That's because I was approaching the problem in an academic manner; in particular, I kept trying to play with one hand what he plays with two, by crossing his arms or by passing the phrase from one hand to the other as he plays it. And finally, when he strikes the keys, his fingers are not curved, but are extended like mallets. This position may cause him to lose speed, especially for the passage of the thumb, but it opens the door to new and innumerable percussive possibilities. And at a time when all the pianists were practicing in order to play with maximum speed, and were creating a new piano academy under the inspiration of Art Tatum and the aegis of Bud Powell, Monk was inventing a new approach to the instrument. Many witnesses have confirmed that, at the beginning of his career, Monk had perfectly satisfactory piano dexterity for the high standards of the times. Griffin even claims that he heard him play entire phrases of Art Tatum, after which Monk immediately added, "But I'm not interested in playing like that. It's just an imitation."

That's how ambiguous Monk's relationships were with his accompanists—they were forced to hear in his style something which encroached upon their own. It was up to them to find their own place in order to complete his music in a personal and pertinent way, without having to change their style. This as a big challenge: to maintain the difficult balance between extreme attentiveness to the pianist, and the immediate expression of their own personality. Monk always enjoyed teasing his friends and colleagues, and his subtlety made it all the more formidable.

Saxophonist Steve Lacy tells of being at Monk's home one day and of suddenly seeing a white rabbit run across the room (obviously one of the children's pets).

"Hey, a rabbit," he said.

"What rabbit?" said Thelonious.

"That rabbit, there!"

"What are you talking about, there's no rabbit there," replied Monk boldly.

Lacy realized that Monk was pulling his leg, so he said no more and waited to see what would happen. But nothing happened. Monk simply continued to ignore the rabbit's existence. Lacy said this was the kind of trick Monk loved to play. He tested you to see if you were really sure of yourself, and rarely let on that it was a joke. In Monk's presence, you had to be pretty damn self-confident.

That is one of the earliest characteristics of Monk's music: the delicate combination, required of his sidemen, of confidence and finesse. And he picked the finest drummers to play in his bands: Max Roach, Roy Haynes, Kenny Clarke, or Philly Joe Jones. The same is true for the bassists: Oscar Pettiford, Wilbur Ware, Percy Heath. In music as in love, for reasons which remain more or less mysterious, a particular affinity develops between two musicians which is deep and lasting. It's always hard to explain it after the fact. It depends as much on the music as on the personalities, on the shared adventures— in short, on life. That's the way it is. You can analyze all you want, or list numerous coincidences, but you always come back to the same evidence of perfection. Ahmad Jamal–Vernell Fournier. Miles Davis–Philly Joe Jones. John Coltrane–Elvin Jones. Clifford Brown–Max Roach: the list is endless. The musicians to be pitied are those who go through life alone, never meeting the kindred spirit who can reveal them to the world and to themselves. Those who are already complete, who don't need that little spark, the ones who are condemned to parthenogenesis—it's sad! And as dense, modern, and unique as Thelonious's contribution to music is, it is gratifying to see that the rhythmic expression of this genius was shared generously by Art Blakey.

Art was tough. Born in Pittsburgh two years and a day after Thelonious, at the age of twenty he escaped from the proletarian nightmare of the Carnegie Steel Mill to

786.10524

4745 050

1947

Date	Title								

go with the Fletcher Henderson band—the best thing that could have happened to him. And the worst thing as well, for while on tour through the South in 1941, he was cornered by two cops in Atlanta and beaten up so badly that he said he had to have a steel plate set in his skull. A similar thing happened to Bud Powell, which tragically affected his destiny. In Blakey's case, however, it had—if I may—a galvanizing effect. And when he came to New York in late '42, Max Roach confides, he was already a star and everybody wanted him in their band. This wild man of the drums arrived on 52nd Street, backing up the great pianist Mary Lou Williams, who was also from Pittsburgh. The young Blakey couldn't have had a better credential. In 1942, mainly in Kansas City with the Andy Kirk "Clouds of Joy" Band, her reputation had grown and she began to lead her own trio. She brought her protégé to New York with her and they wound up playing at Kelly's Stable which was, along with the Three Deuces, the Onyx, and the Famous Door, one of the pillars of 52nd Street, "the street that never slept," as it was advertised. The young drummer was a sensation, and that is most likely when he met Monk. And then, from 1944 to 1946, he was at the heart of the bebop revolution, in the Billy Eckstine band. Over the months, one great trumpet player followed another: Dizzy Gillespie, Miles Davis, Fats Navarro, and Kenny Dorham. On saxophone: Charlie Parker, Gene Ammons, Dexter Gordon, Lucky Thompson, and Leo Parker. On bass, Tommy Potter, and on piano and arrangements, Tadd Dameron. Plus Sarah Vaughan. What a band! A beehive! They were all there. Bird playing scales from the back of the bus, Miles looking for the sound which would make him famous, each of them furiously seeking to discover what fate had in store. Blakey was one of them, and his association with Monk was just a matter of time. He hadn't played in the Minton's sessions with Charlie Christian. He had never accompanied Coleman Hawkins, the master pilot of jazz history; he hadn't payed the dues in the clubs and studios like Max Roach; he hadn't orchestrated the new music like Tadd Dameron. He had simply come to town, and that was enough: he was Art Blakey, jazz drummer. He didn't challenge Kenny Clarke, his fellow Pittsburgh compatriot, five years his senior, about the new drumming style which played the four beats on the cymbal and left the bass drum free to "drop bombs" at the right moment. He didn't have the brilliant percussive concepts of Max Roach, or the calm and precocious wisdom of Shadow Wilson. Art Blakey, jazz drummer. Brand-new, fresh out of the gate, he had fantastic swing, energy, and musicality. As saxophonist Ike Quebec said, "other drummmers make a thump," but Art goes POW!" He was in big demand. And that's how Monk came to make some unbelievable tracks with him on his first recordings for Blue Note in 1947. It is their first official, documented meeting.

By a chance of fate (and thanks to producer Alan Bates's intuition), Blakey was there when Monk recorded his last trio in London in 1971 for Black Lion Records: a magnificent pause in the form of da capo which brought to an end a quarter century of superlative collaboration. Something magical, and palpable, existed between these two men. They shared the same sense of immediate authority, and of instinctive percussion. They fit together, like a puzzle.

One story in particular reveals the ferocious but affectionate relationship between Art and Thelonious. The Baroness Pannonica de Koenigswarter, of whom we shall learn more later, had never met Thelonious's wife, Nellie. As a good friend of Blakey's at the time, she came to hear him in a club where his band was playing, with Monk on piano. She sat down at a table with Nellie, who had come to listen to her husband. She introduced herself and said she was pleased to hear that there were no more money problems. "How's that?" said Nellie, astounded. "Yes," replied the Baroness, "this arrangement must be working out okay for you." "What did you say?" answered Nellie, even more surprised. They talked it over, and it turned out that Blakey had convinced Pannonica of the fact that Monk, who was a little mad (you just had to see him to believe it), only rarely brought the money home from the gig. This was a subtle lie, for Thelonious was one of the few musicians who *always* brought his money home. Blakey had persuaded the Baroness to drive him to Monk's place each night so he could, according to him, hand the money directly over to Nellie. He would just take a walk around the block, then get back in the car, thus doubling his night's pay in a few minutes. Monk liked him too much to hold it against him, and from then on would just keep an eye on him when it came to money matters. The only conflict I ever heard of between them concerned Nica— Thelonious reproached Art for not treating her with all due respect.

They were exemplary friends. In the early sixties, writer and journalist Joe Goldberg described Blakey's apartment on Central Park West as that of someone who had made a lot of money, and who spent it with good taste. The only detail which revealed that it was a musician's home was the wall by the telephone: it was covered with photographs of Thelonious Monk.

‖ 4 ‖

Women

There were also women in Thelonious's life. In fact, he was surrounded by them, like a tight fence that protected him from the hecticism of the world. The cliché image of the jazz musician as ill-shaven, trying to pick up some chick in a bar in Cleveland, while wondering where he's going to get the money to pay his third wife's alimony, doesn't apply in Thelonious's case. The brief list of those who protected his vital privacy includes his mother, Barbara; his sister Marion; Nellie, his wife; and Pannonica, his patroness. A biographer's nightmare, for beyond this limit there was no access to the man. Monk was never a womanizer—far from it. And that's probably why his women surrounded him with such special affection.

There are as many women in the jazz world as anywhere else, so why is it we never hear about them? There had to have been a few whose talent finally got recognized, and of course there were the singers, but that's not the point here. Surely in jazz there must be some

Cosima Wagners, some George Sands or some Anna Magdelana Bachs—women who were either companions, muses, harlots, or precious treasures. Either there is a lack of biographies in this field, or the world of swing is particularly macho (why more than elsewhere?). In fact, we tend to think of jazz musicians' wives like the wives of sailors. A flash of love, followed by the nesting instinct; then some more-or-less gifted children, and for their husbands' other needs, there are places that specialize. In short, jazz is the business of men, and not very clean men at that. The wife only comes out of hiding after the great genius dies, to claim her just dues, and to prevent a band from using her husband's name. It is not very exciting, nor very exact—but people remember gossip, and then again, dignified women don't usually make headline news.

And as for dignity, Nellie has plenty of it. She and Thelonious once made a mutual agreement to never speak in public of one another, either alive or dead. This was both a token of esteem and an awareness of the media's capacity to meddle in their private life. So ever since Thelonious's death, she hasn't given a single interview, she isn't writing any sensational memoirs, and has never forbid anyone from doing anything. She now enjoys the honors and privileges of a well-filled life. Ever since the age of twelve, when she first met Thelonious, her life began to move quickly, and it has never stopped.

It seems that it all started on a basketball court. Nellie's family had just moved into the neighborhood—over on 62nd Street—and her big brother, who was Monk's age, started looking for friends to play in the street with. One night he came home and said, "I met this kid from 63rd Street who's a great basketball player." "Oh, yeah?" replied Nellie. "And he's a monster piano player." "Yeah . . . ?" "And you know what his name is? Thelonious Monk!" Nellie just had to go over and check him out. It was love at first sight, but it took fifteen years for them to come together, as they were married in 1947. A fine example of perseverance. If you put it that way, it sounds like she finally hooked him after years of trying. In fact, it looks more like he hooked *her*, and for life. At the time, Nellie was too young for Thelonious to be interested in her. In any case, it wouldn't have been proper. And then, his older sister Marion had girlfriends who were undoubtedly more tempting for the young Thelonious. So nothing happened between them for a long time, which enabled them to become friends. As she was his buddy's sister, they got to know each other first as friends, not as lovers. Gradually, their mutual attraction grew stronger and deeper, and by the end of the 1930s, they were together—for good.

Their separate roles were quickly established. Thelonious made music, and Nellie did all the rest—literally all the rest. Which meant taking care of the house (which, it's true, wasn't very big); the mother-in-law (who died in the fall of 1953); their two children Thelonious and Barbara (born in 1949 and 1952), and her husband Thelonious, who played piano, watched TV while eating ice cream, or lay on the couch and argued with friends who'd stop by. She had to bring in money for this little brood, as he couldn't feed the family with his Blue Note or Prestige royalties. Don't forget, either (we'll come back to this), that after Monk had his cabaret card revoked in 1951, he was forbidden to play in New York City until 1957. And as Monk hardly ever left New York, it was not gig money that would keep his family going. So Nellie did housework, took in sewing, and did overtime—

sometimes working three jobs a day—and never complained.

Now, just imagine a woman whose good sense outweighs her love for her husband. If we happened to eavesdrop on the Monk family one night, back in late 1952, here's what we might have heard:

1. I'm sick and tired of your mother.

2. The only thing you ever do around the house is drink beer with your so-called friends.

3. You can't get a job 'cause you lost your cabaret card—and just so you could protect that Bud Powell, who'll never be anything but trouble, and who'll wind up in the gutter anyway.

4. We already have one child, and here I am pregnant again. How are we going to feed them?

5. Your records don't sell because you won't make the least concession to your Art, which people couldn't care less about. Your friend Dizzy's name is in all the papers, and even little Miles Davis is starting to make some serious money. How come you—the one they all respect — can't make a dime, and in the papers they can't even get your name straight?

6. Meanwhile I'm wasting the best years of my life, and breaking my back so that Mister Cool can play the cult hero.

7. I've had it. I'm going back to my mother.

This typical scene must have been played out in any number of jazzmen's homes; their life expectancy as a couple rarely went beyond the arrival of the second child. But this could never be the case in Monk's home, because Nellie understood from the beginning what her love for, and confidence in, Thelonious would cost her.

Perhaps she was more convinced of his genius than even he was, and knew the sacrifices he'd have to make to gain the world's recognition. So, simply, she just went on doing what had to be done. Thelonious was well aware of this, and devoted himself entirely to his music. This was serious teamwork in the fight to come.

On my right, weighing in at 320 pounds, and no savings account—Mr. and Mrs. Monk. On my left, New York City, the crusher, the destroyer of dreams and destinies. In this 15-round main event, the odds were stacked against them. Nellie knew all this, and did everything she could with dignity and patience to achieve a victory.

She always stuck by her husband, at home when times were tough, and on the road when his career started to take off. This tall, lean, willowy woman picked out his clothes, ordered his meals, kept track of the gig money and concerts, packed his bags, sent postcards, called for cabs, dealt with the producers and organizers, unpacked his bags, worried about being late, turned down con men and dubious propositions, paid the extra charges and re-packed his bags. She took care of it all. Everything had to go through her and whoever was near Thelonious knew it. His confidence in her was absolute and blind, and the idea of leaving New York without her was unthinkable. If she didn't go, then neither did he.

And as he gradually became ill, the pressure increased, because now she had to protect him from himself. His son tells of what it felt like standing in front of a man who couldn't recognize his own children. The child's reaction is to flee this vision of horror. But Nellie's problem was to get them to understand that they had to face that reality. As young as they were, it was up to them to look after their father, just as he looked after them when he was able to. A huge amount of love and confidence is needed to counterbalance that ever-threatening storm-cloud. And Nellie was just that balance.

Today, there is a new generation of motorboats called "cigarette boats," whose motor is much too powerful for the hull of the boat. Because of their high speed and tenuous balance, they can flip in a second in a rough sea. So they are equipped with a movable ballast mechanism which moves from fore to aft in the boat to keep it balanced. The whole trick is knowing just where to set it. And that was Nellie: always on deck and constantly trying to keep that enormous creative power on an even keel, a power carrying the whole family headlong towards either success, or catastrophe. She had to position herself exactly, and every instant was critical.

It was more than difficult, for Thelonious Monk was a little "weird." Some policeman, for example, in a southern state would see him walking down the street with his arms spread out like an airplane, and call him over. In cases like this, Thelonious didn't say a thing, and just rolled his fearsome eyes. And what does the grassroots racist from Mississippi see? An imposing, heavyset black man with a strange look in his eyes, oblivious, seemingly borderline crazy, wearing a bizarre hat, and who suddenly refuses to make the slightest movement. At best, the cop pulls out his club and whacks him, which happened to him more than once. At worst, he draws his gun and shoots him. That's the catastrophe scenario that Nellie was forced to anticipate every day, and it was exhausting. Daily life is lived on the edge, and Thelonious could always step over it much too easily.

The trouble with Monk was that when he came up against aggression, he physically withdrew into himself with a sort of violence in reverse, which was as dangerous as if he used it to throw a punch or shout an insult. This was a huge responsibility for Nellie, as she had to act in the dual roles of mother and wife. Each day she had to justify, defuse, and protect the man, Thelonious, who had his mind on only two things: his family and his music. Which is why Nellie was so relieved when she received the precious assistance and friendship of Pannonica. It was all a little too much for one woman.

Baroness Pannonica de Koenigswarter was certainly out of the ordinary. As the daughter of Lord Rothschild—the English branch of the family—she, like her brothers and sisters, was born into a life of privilege and honor. And there wasn't the slightest doubt that a magnificent and noble marriage would perpetuate the Rothschild legacy. However, her first name alone, Pannonica, seemed to destine her to a life of originality and eccentricity, a life for which her family would constantly reproach her. And yet, it was her father, a lepidopterist, who, discovering an unknown species of butterfly in the region of central Europe known today as Hungary, but once called Pannonia, decided to give the name both to the butterfly and to his daughter. When the time came, she married a dashing aristocratic young officer in the French army, the Baron Jules de Koenigswarter, who, in that pre–World War II period, seemed destined for glory. They were made for each other.

Yet, there was never a couple more alike and dissimilar at the same time. Born into the same aristocratic background, their union seemed natural enough, but everything drew them apart. He was stern, dour, serious and responsible. He was only interested in arts of the martial variety, and his *honneur* held sway over his sense of humor. By marrying Nica, this fine man entered a world which at first seemed familiar, but was in fact completely foreign. She was imaginative, artistic (a talented painter and pianist), unconcerned with convention and propriety, the youngest of the family, and not the least bit disposed to fulfill the social functions for which her upbringing had prepared her. In short, she was an original. He was bored at concerts, and she found dinner parties tedious. Yet, the profound love they shared united them and was enough to transform their differences into mutual adoration.

Then came the war. Young Jules answered the call of General de Gaulle, and the young couple moved to England. Jules then took part in the African campaign at the head of an armored unit, and Nica was said to have joined the *maquis*, driving ambulances, following her husband into combat, and working devotedly for the Resistance as a nurse. I couldn't verify the story, but as long as it seems plausible, why not accept it without quibbling?

After the war, Jules entered the diplomatic corps. He and Nica had six children and everything seemed to promise an exciting and cosmopolitan life. But, sadly, things began to crack.

While stationed in New York on assignment, Jules noticed that through Nica's love of art and music, she was adopting some of the behavioral habits and vices of those he referred to as "her Negro friends." She was not exactly the ideal wife for a diplomat. She tended to dress carelessly, and detested having to receive a constant crowd of superficial and self-seeking people. She smoked marijuana, and conducted herself in the most unbecoming way for the wife of an official in the public eye. Both of their families felt sorry for poor Jules, who was then faced with the choice between his wife and his career.

He finally made up his mind to leave his wife, remarry, and continue his diplomatic career. Nica stayed in New York, where her passion for jazz kept her riveted. It goes without saying that because of her inadmissable behavior, her family prevented her from handling the family portfolio and cut her off from much of the Rothschild millions. Even so, if you are a Rothschild, you still get to keep two Bentleys and a Rolls-Royce, buy a magnificent home on the New Jersey side of the Hudson River with a panoramic view of Manhattan, and take care of two hundred or so cats.

For a jazz musician, who spends half his time trying to keep his head above water, both financially and legally, you can imagine the impression the Baroness made when her limousine quietly pulled up to the Village Vanguard, and invested that holy place with an exquisitely luxurious perfume. Because that's why Nica was there—to remind these great artists, who had devoted their lives to their instruments, that there exists a splendor and a standing which genius deserves. Charlie Parker spent the end of his life going between clubs, standing on sordid street corners where dealers, or cops, or both, were waiting for him, and the pawn shop where he'd hocked his horn a score of times. The door to Pannonica's room at the Hotel Stanhope was the last one left open to him, so he could die in peace, and not in the street. Monk spent almost his whole life in a tiny, cluttered apartment. And it was also to Nica's—but this time in Weehawken— where he and Nellie decided to go into a ten-year exile to get some peace and quiet which Manhattan did not afford.

Nica had class. Whoever met her was immediately impressed by her aristocratic temperance, humanity, and elegance. She was a breath of fresh air in that stifling

New York jazz jungle. For the musicians, she provided a sense of dignity, and the hope of being recognized as someone useful and admirable by a society which was either indifferent or hostile. In short, being with Nica was like being in high society.

And she gave Thelonious and his family some things Nellie never could: a whole army of lawyers to help him regain his cabaret card when it was briefly revoked for a second time, in 1950; the top floor of a huge house where he and his wife could spend their older days; a Steinway piano to compose and practice on; the use of her Bentley. And on top of all that, she gave him a friendship of infinite affection and respect. There was no question of a rivalry with Nellie. Nothing even like that. She simply offered her time, her money, and her patience, when Nellie had difficulties dealing with the attacks of silent agitation that Thelonious suffered from more and more frequently. Nica was always there to recommend doctors, or hospitals, or treatments—to watch, to worry and to advise.

Let's get one thing straight: I don't see Nica as a saint. You don't go directly from the international aristocratic set to the jazz clubs without getting a few scars. And for anyone in the know, she must have looked like the archetype of what we now call a "bourgeois hippie." Her privileged upbringing surely blinded her to many of the harsh realities of life, and occasionally made her seem somewhat ludicrous. Many times when the pressure was on, because of her great admiration for Thelonious, she would try to take care of his affairs. But her efforts met with little success, as might be expected. And then, too, there were the drugs, which ravage even the loveliest women.

Nevertheless, she was a flamboyant personality who

shone over her contemporaries with unequaled passion and generosity. She was a kind of pixilated fairy godmother, whose mere presence was a reminder that music is beautiful, and that honor is not in vain—an eccentric but benevolent sign of some kind of divine justice. She was a benefactress, a patroness of the arts, who came from a world devoid of need and worry.

But this was misleading, as she paid for this freespiritedness, and with heavy interest. She paid for it with her marriage (although she remained close to her husband right up to her death), and was cut off from her family and friends. Through her devotion to jazz, she committed social suicide. Even if she remained financially well-off, her position must have been a daily reminder of the exclusion she shared with her musician friends. They were profoundly grateful, and proved it with the only form of wealth they possessed—their music. Monk dedicated his magnificent eponymous composition "Pannonica," to her. And there were many others, including the subtle "Nica's Tempo" by Gigi Gryce (one version exists with Monk on piano), "Blues for Nica" by Kenny Drew, "Tonica" by Kenny Dorham, Tommy Flanagan's "Thelonica," and the famous "Nica's Dream" by Horace Silver.

There is no counting the number of musicians and musicians' families she helped, understood, and supported. She was much more than some kind of eccentric character in the mad drama of the New York jazz scene: for many people she represented love, hope, or simply survival. But in the integrity and faith of the Monk family, she seemed to have found the exact equivalent of her European aristocracy. Their values were so different, and yet so similar. Thelonious de Monk—a true aristocrat of the spirit.

And it's strange to see how Nica has gone down in history: two of the world's most famous jazz musicians, Charlie Parker and Thelonious Monk, died at her home. Reality is infinitely varied and lively, but history is ruthless and often only registers the graves of people and events. Nica's relationship with Charlie Parker was one of a generous woman trying to help a man who was desperate. There was not the same intensity or the same respect as in her relationship with Monk. Bird died at her place almost by accident; Monk, by affection.

The perfect illustration of Monk's relationship with the Baroness can be seen in an anecdote told by saxophonist Barney Wilen who played on the soundtrack of Roger Vadim's movie, *Les liaisons dangereuses* (1960). Monk had been called in as bandleader, and he and Nica drove down to the recording session in her Bentley, through the pouring rain. When they reached the studio, Monk was disturbed that he hadn't received any of the preliminary contracts for the session, and refused to get out of the car until he had them. Nica went in to talk it over with the producers. She returned, in the rain, and explained to Thelonious, ensconced in the Bentley, that the problem was being worked out and everything would be all right. He kept refusing, and she kept running back and forth. Soaked to the skin, Nica pleaded through the window, "I assure you, Thelonious, the man looks honest to me, please come in." As it turned out, Monk finally went in and played, but the producer was never able to get the rights to the soundtrack, and could not get a record made of it. It is now known under the name of Art Blakey. Nica was well-intentioned, but Monk was right.

It is unjust to call Nica the jazz musician's gravedigger. By a strange stroke of fate, even her own death coincided with that of another person who was very close to Monk, Charlie Rouse. But I see her more as a foreigner who, like Lion and Wolff whom we will meet later, hears something in Monk's music which the American ear did not seem to pick up. Normalcy is something ambiguous in the United States, where nonconformity is often the sign of something new, potentially interesting and profitable. But it often takes the eye of a foreigner, a European, an ancestor, to recognize genius in originality, and beauty in strangeness. The contribution of jazz, and of black culture in general, to American civilization is a vast subject which has been studied and described by numerous scholars. But one thing is certain: America has trouble accepting the existence of jazz unless it is watered down, digested and cut off from its roots. This is part of the old melting-pot illlusion. Nica (along with a few others) was an outsider to this problem, so her sense of national pride was not involved, and her vision of the young Thelonious was not clouded by any racism whatsoever.

I know very little about Thelonious's mother, Barbara. She is the one who made the move to 243 West 63rd Street, where the Monk family would reside for almost fifty years, even after her death. She was a strong-willed woman who raised her three children by herself. From the start, she believed in her son's musical talent, and encouraged him to pursue a career which many mothers would have considered too unstable and immoral to guarantee a decent future for a family. In midlife she decided to convert to a demanding, extremist religion and became a Jehovah's Witness, and converted Thomas, her other son. I see her as a woman of great conviction, with a sense of honor, who instilled two values which would guide the members of her family throughout their lives: those of love and dignity. Thelonious was very close to his mother, and he was her favorite. It is likely that her death in late 1953 opened the way to the mental problems he began to suffer beginning in 1954. Her memory was perpetuated by Monk's daughter Barbara who was born at that time and named for her grandmother.

More is known of this Barbara. She was nicknamed Boo-Boo and was the only woman of a younger generation to play an influential part in Monk's world. Her name perpetuated the spirit of her grandmother. According to all who knew her, she was always very close to her father, and had inherited his gift for music. She had more in common with Thelonious than simply being able to play his compositions at an early age, for she soon revealed herself to be just as intense as he, and as brusque, laconic, and able to stun by a single remark. She saw and understood everything, but said nothing—definitely her father's daughter.

One example comes to mind which illustrates their family resemblance. Have you noticed how Monk plays his introductions? Most of the time, the few bars a pianist usually plays before the band comes in can say a lot about the man. There's the "standard" method of playing the end of the tune, in order to prime the "swing" pump, and to get the band off on the right track. There's the subtle method of creating a tasteful cadence, which sketches the color of the tune in the background. Then there's the percussive approach, consisting of playing a small rhythmic phrase, repeated over four bars, as an appetizer served before the main feast of the tune. Or there's the austere approach—just two or three notes of a chord. Each piano player has his own way of introducing the music.

But you don't often hear intros like Monk's. His melodies are angular though familiar, and even when he refers to a well-known tune, he makes it sound like something new. You might think he should take the edge off it (but why should he take the edge off anything?), take us diplomatically by the ear and lead us step by step into his musical world. But no, Monk cuts right to the heart of the matter. He carefully chooses the one phrase, the most abrupt and hermetic one in the whole tune and serves it up, still wrapped and fastened with a knot on its special little plate. It's a small creature with an undefinable shape that crawls up your eardrum, and tickles a part of your brain you thought had been asleep for the past million years. Slip over to your stack of records and listen to the introduction to "Gallop's Gallop," with Gigi Gryce (*Nica's Tempo*, Signal, 1955)—it's abstract enough to set your teeth on edge. Or else "I Let a Song Go Out of My Heart" (*Monk Plays Duke Ellington*, Riverside, 1955) which, by grabbing the tail end of the melody and running it through the Monk mixer, he turns it into something totally enigmatic. With age, Monk gradually abandoned the pleasure of these biting introductions, but right up to the early sixties, they are a true feast for the ears.

I'll never cease to marvel at his opening to the arch-standard "I Should Care," where he is supposed to lead the way for singer Kenny "Pancho" Hagood (*With Milt Jackson*, Blue Note, 1948). This introduction always reminds me of a scene from a Buster Keaton film in which he's at a swimming pool and he wants to impress his girlfriend by his moves on the high diving board. The diver's natural movement (like that of the pianist introducing a tune) is to launch his body (the music) in a progressive and continuous thrust. But Keaton, reaching the end of the board, suddenly terrorized by the height, breaks his fluid motion down into a dozen contradictory and almost simultaneous movements, creating a ballet which blends his momentum and his fear of falling. The effect is one of comic brilliance, and I must have played those two or three seconds back in slow motion at least twenty times in order to study the scene that he surely had to work on for days.

The intro to "I Should Care" works the same way. Don't forget that in such a case you are starting from scratch, and the listener has no rhythmic or harmonic bearings to refer to. That's what the piano is supposed to provide. Well, instead of peacefully stating a key and a tempo, Monk sticks absolutely ambiguous chords in the most incomprehensible places, and the vocalist's entrance then seems nothing short of miraculous. Practically speaking, here's what must have happened: they agreed on a four-bar piano intro, counted off a tempo, then Thelonious just took off. Too bad for anyone who listened to him, instead of concentrating on the infamous four bars! If you got dazzled by his unpredictable acrobatics (which change with each take), you wouldn't come in on time! And without the snap of the fingers counting off the tempo before the tune starts, the listener is thrown headlong into an angular and complex world which both shocks and charms the ear. So it's not surprising that Monk played so little with vocalists. An intro like that is enough to put half of them in a psychiatric ward where they'd still be wondering in their padded cells what the hell had happened. With Monk, you really have to hang on tight.

Nothing in these introductions better represents what

"basic Monk" is than the way he shoots out sideways from the very start—he just can't help it. That is the Monk signature. And that is the signature he handed down intact to his daughter Barbara who was made in his image and molded from the same clay. They were both eccentric, but had the same imposing presence and cast of mind. The surprising thing is that Boo-Boo wanted to become a dancer, then gave it up when she was twenty-five. From then on she concentrated on music, and her brother still remembers how, from the beginning, she had a gift for writing tunes with harmonies strangely like those of her father, with an instinctive melodic confidence. An enchanted royal path lay ahead, and the future seemed to be hers.

She died of cancer at the age of twenty-nine. Following her father to the grave, Barbara's only satisfaction was to have spared him the pain of her own death. Thus Thelonious's near-double died at practically the same time as he, leaving behind an acrid taste of defeat and memory. Of all these primordial women in Monk's life, the only ones alive as I write these lines are his sister Marion, and Nellie, his wife.

‖ 5 ‖

Producers I

There was another woman whose enthusiasm for Thelonious's music helped open doors for him, a woman who was amazed to see that those doors had for so long remained shut. Thirty years old and still no recordings under his own name? How could this be possible? Lorraine Lion couldn't understand. So she put all her youthful energy into getting the pianist recognized by an industry which had always ignored him. But she was different from the women mentioned earlier, for she held a big trump card in the record game: she was the wife of Alfred Lion who, along with Francis Wolff, cofounded the Blue Note record label which a few years later was to play a major role in the history of jazz. Lion had fled Nazi Germany, and in January 1939, founded his record company in the United States, with the sole purpose of recording Albert Ammons and Meade Lux Lewis—two boogie-woogie piano players whose music had filled him with enthusiasm. Gradually, other artists in the same vein began to appear in his catalogue; however, Lion hadn't yet acquired a taste for the music known as be-bop.

At a time when the whole planet was crumbling under the bombs of World War II, the jazz scene in New York was undergoing a similar upheaval. And for the uninformed listener, the bebop war took place on a battlefield which was still difficult to delineate. But already, in 1944, Lion, who had meanwhile joined Wolff, was becoming interested in a "modern" saxophonist by the name of Ike Quebec, who began to record for them. That was a foot in the door. Quebec introduced Lion to a host of musicians who were soon to make up "the Blue Note team," and who would quickly make the label one of the hottest on the jazz scene.

Thelonious was one of the first musicians introduced to Lion and the producer was immediately enchanted. He loved Monk's music, and gave him a five-year exclusive contract. In so doing he was fullfilling his promise to recognize and promote the talent of exceptional musicians. Despite the passive or, at times, contemptuous indifference of the critics, Lion and Wolff continued to stand up for Monk, paying him out of their own pockets. They were convinced that their man was one of the century's great geniuses. In the business, people were saying that their artistic policy would lead to commercial suicide. The future, however, proved the Blue Note producers right, but at the time their only capital was their convictions. They were, indeed, truly great producers.

There have been all kinds of jazz producers: the courageous, the business-minded, the crooked, the visionaries, the jazz lovers, the cautious, the suicidal, the ruined, and the millionaires. We've seen them all! Perhaps we should take a closer look at them. For without them, nothing gets done, and it would be a mistake to ignore them.

There are several different types. In the early 1950s, there were the executive producers, the producers, and then the famous A&R men (for "artists and repertory"). An executive producer is, above all, concerned with money, which means that to record an artist, he invests certain funds which he expects to get back (and make a profit) when the recording is sold. Which means that, since he provides the money, he reserves the right to choose the musicians and the context. The producer, then, takes care of the other requirements, such as booking the studio, contacting the musicians and making sure they get to the right place on the right day, ordering pizza for the break; in short, doing everything possible to make sure the session goes as smoothly as possible. This is a very important stage, because a jazz record is nothing more than a fleeting instance of the artist's music, captured on one single day of his life. One day earlier or later would produce completely different results. There are magical sessions, and there are also total flops. And it is possible to set up a magical session, by the choice of the musicians, the tunes, the sound engineer, and the rest—this is all the producer's job. It also requires a great deal of intelligence and intuition during a session to bring out the full potential of the music. The producer has to make suggestions with discretion and tact, know when to go on to the next tune, feel when the session is getting bogged down in a tricky number, find a last-minute replacement when necessary (often the case in the history of jazz), keep everybody cool when a technical problem arises, (and God knows they alway do)—"Sounds like a problem with the mikes; hold on a second, I want to check something. . . ."—just when you were about record the perfect take. And above all he has to find the most diplomatic way to portray the artist's natural enemy: the money man.

Then there are the A&R men. As their name indicates, their responsibility is for both the choice of musicians and for the color of the music that they offer to the label employing them. And here another distinction should be made (the last one, I promise) between the independent or small labels, and the majors.

The small independent labels have a dozen artists whose work sells fairly well. They aim at a specific audience and produce a hit every now and then. The profits are small, considering the extent of the catalog. In the early fifties, a major was usually a profitable and diversified branch of a large company (Columbia or RCA Victor), or a label which had big name stars of vocal or instrumental jazz—Capitol had Nat King Cole, Sinatra, and George Shearing; Decca had Louis Armstrong and Ella Fitzgerald. You find the A&R men in these companies acting as artistic directors. They don't invest in the operation, as they are on salary, but they are fired if the records they're in charge of don't sell.

However, for the small companies like Blue Note, the executive producer and the producer are the same person. They have to be, in order to keep an eye on their investment each step of the way, and to supervise the quality both in the studio and in the front office—which makes a huge difference in some cases. Then there is the category of independent producers who are contracted and who receive a percentage on the sales for the small or, more often, the bigger labels, as was the case for Teo Macero, Monk's producer at Columbia.

I'll round off this gallery of portraits by removing the veil of mystery which surrounds the agent. His job is to look after the artist's business and defend his interests—finding, then negotiating contracts for clubs, or record companies, talking to the press for him, and in general serving as a kind of screen between the musician and the rest of the world. (Monk took on an agent, but that was later, in 1955.) Once again, one man can be both producer and agent, as was the case with Norman Granz who organized concerts and tours (the famous "Jazz at the Philharmonic"), and recorded artists on one of his several labels (Clef, Norgran, Verve, then Pablo).

It's obvious that this listing masks a much simpler reality. Basically, there are two men—one whose job is to make music, the other to sell it. And both their lives depend on how well this relationship works out. It's important to understand this, for Thelonious did not have what would be considered a "normal" behavior pattern. He wasn't flexible. He understood perfectly the various economic constraints, but chose to ignore them whenever they got in his way. He always had a very precise idea of what he wanted, and, like all visionaries, he had trouble convincing those who weren't already on his side. And he rarely tried. His rapport with his different producers is a perfect illustration of the gap that existed between his genius and his ability to sell it.

Thelonious's recording career began with brio. In five years and seven sessions (the first three spread over only two months), Monk recorded thirty-three tunes for Alfred and Lorraine Lion which came out at the time on fifteen 78 rpm records, and three collections on 10-inch records. The label certainly didn't cut corners.

And Monk was turning tunes out abundantly—twenty-three original compositions. And not the lesser ones either. They included future classics such as "Round Midnight," "Straight, No Chaser," and "Ruby,

My Dear." Then there were others which he never re-corded again—"Humph," "Who Knows," "Skippy," "Hornin' In," and "Sixteen." Without even mentioning the ones he most likely wrote in that period, then only recorded later, such as "Bye-Ya" and "Rhythm-a-ning." You can imagine how excited the Lions were to discover this musical monument! A meteorite had fallen into their garden! The mysterious stone, the star of wonder!

Monk's first session for them, as is often the case for a first job, was a little confused. That was less because of Thelonious's fault, than Ike Quebec's, his mentor at Blue Note. For Quebec used the session to insert two of his own compositions, half of the four tunes they re-corded that day. Don't forget the royalties. And as noth-ing is for free, those were the dues you had to pay to go into the studio. Monk played Quebec's tunes with the same integrity as he played his own, but when you think of what he had in store . . .

And then starting off with a sextet is just asking for trouble. That means a lot of people in the studio, a lot of musical conventions to be respected, and a lot of wrong starts and missed count-offs. When you lack re-cording experience, it only makes things worse.

But none of that was a serious problem, for Monk led everyone along with his usual, ever-present confidence and aplomb. He was sure of himself, right from the very first note of the first tune of his first session. His presence was so strong that it eclipsed the confusion reigning in the studio. And, what's more, the two compositions he brought along were brilliantly original. When asked the title of the first, he grumbled, with his usual loquacious-ness, "Humph . . ."

And that is how that onomatopoeia became classified

as a Thelonious Monk composition. For the second, the title was already set: "Thelonious." There was his very signature on the record.

And the band was made up of first-rate musicians: Art Blakey, his buddy, who joyfully inaugurated his twenty-five years of recording with Thelonious; Gene Ramey on bass, who had come up from Kansas City with Charlie Parker in the Jay McShann orchestra; trumpet player Idriss Sulieman and saxophonist Billy Smith. Even Danny Quebec West, the nephew Ike suggested for the session, although only seventeen, turned out to be a solid and inventive alto player.

Just over a month later, Monk had his second session. Now no longer a recording novice, he was able to deliver the full measure of his genius, this time in trio. Among friends, with Art Blakey and Gene Ramey. Two standards, "Nice Work If You Can Get It," and "April in Paris," seemed to have been written just for him. Also included were a delicious ballad, "Ruby, My Dear," a medium tempo but exuberant "Well You Needn't," and two spellbinding tunes, "Introspection" and "Off Minor," which to this day remain enigmas of modernity. This was high art, and the session was one of exceptional cohesion and facility. The music being played was so miraculous that the session was extended from the originally planned four tunes to six. The next month, the same thing. With his quintet this time, Monk raised the stakes even higher, with "In Walked Bud," "Monk's Mood," "Round Midnight," and "Who Knows," the session's only concession to the mad-paced, infernal tempos played by the boppers.

By the end of 1947, Lion had fourteen titles recorded with various groups, and all of them were excellent. And when they decided to put them on the market, they should have had every reason to celebrate. Monk was thirty years old. Welcome to planet Mars.

So much has been said about Ornette Coleman's record *Free Jazz*, which in a single track shook the entire world of jazz music. And these first recordings by Monk were just as explosive and should have produced the same effect. But it is not enough to just drop a bomb; you have to be sure it doesn't fall in a desert. For the record buyers at the time were not ready to have their ears bent in such a radical way. Let's just call it a time bomb.

On the records, everything is already there—matured, carefully thought-out, and finely crafted. Three and a half minutes of pure genius. There aren't too many musicians who come on the scene already complete. There's always the formative period, when you can get a sense of the great artist despite his early awkward attempts. The smart producer gets excited, senses a good deal, and signs up the artist who is still a little green. But Thelonious was the opposite. When he showed up with his little pictures, they were all ready to be hung on the wall for the exhibition. Also, having begun recording so late in life allowed him to mature in his corner, where only the initiates would notice him. But the most important thing about these recordings is that he immediately established himself as a composer. By offering variable groups, trio, quintet, and sextet, he was able to reveal the vitality of his genius in each of these combinations. He didn't put himself forward like a virtuoso, even though he was one in his own unique way. The music he was possessed with was expressed through the piano, but it seemed to find its natural extension in other instruments, too, which, instead of casting a shadow on his own style, served rather to underline its extreme and radical originality.

Shortly after his death, a record was made by a group of Monk's admirers, entitled *That's the Way I Feel Now.* Musicians of all kinds, but mainly from pop and rock, took part in this homage entirely devoted to Monk's compositions. But not only within a jazz format, but also electric guitars, synthesizers, rock drums, the whole sha-bam. These people all play Monk's tunes almost note for note, and it's both instructive and wonderful to realize that even in a completely different context, his music sounds as amazingly fresh as ever. And it will still sound that way ten centuries from now played on instruments you can hardly imagine, like laser harps, transubstantial polyphonias, who knows what, as long as it is played exactly as he wrote it.

Monk usually spent several weeks writing a tune, playing it relentlessly, ad nauseum, until he got the final version. He spun and wove ceaselessly at the loom of his genius. There he sat in the tiny apartment, at the upright piano, the floor beneath it worn away by the soles of his shoes. Sketch it, draw it, paint it, there you have it. Monk's pieces are the complete opposite of the flighty and polymorphous compositions that can be played in different tempos, or in various keys. Whether with a big band, solo, trio or quartet, Monk always plays the same thing, and it is up to everybody else to follow him!

Take his composition "Shuffle Boil." Without going into technical detail, the two high notes in the melody are just out of the tenor saxophone range. They can be played, but only by using the overtones of the instrument, which are difficult to control, and can sometimes produce awkward squeaks. The sax player's first reaction: Listen, man, you wrote this too high; you mind if

I play it down an octave? Monk: You're a professional musician, right? You got your union card, right? Then play the motherfucker the way I wrote it.

That's all there was to it. And the wildest thing is that Monk is right! The sound was there! Despite the false notes, or because of them! The revenge of mind over matter!

Even more than painting, his work reminds me of sculpture. Monk composes with a burin and a chisel. Each time he plays a note, it's as if a little shard of marble flies off. It's almost painful, but you realize you're on your way toward the perfect form, angular but smooth—not like Miles Davis or Ahmad Jamal who sensually caress the idea of a melody idea, or Art Tatum who reveals all the different possibilites at once in a kind of epileptic vision. Monk reminds me of Brancusi—he sculpts big, upright, compact pieces out of the sound mass which, when they are finished, dazzle you with their beauty, their rigor, and their humor.

As for tempo, let it be known immediately: Monk's compositions have *one* specific tempo, sometimes two, but they're always the same. He leaves it up to others to turn "Round Midnight" into a ballad (which it originally was not), or "Well, You Needn't" into an uptempo tune (which it wasn't, either). Using a metronome, I investigated the possible tempo variations of some of his tunes, throughout his whole recording career. The verdict? Aside from a few rare exceptions, the tempo doesn't budge a hair. He hears his compositions at one tempo, just like there's usually only one way to play a certain chord behind the melody. This is almost unheard-of in jazz—the ultimate protean musical form—for jazz constantly chews up and digests its repertory in order to transform it.

I was speaking of Miles Davis. Look at what he does to his famous "All Blues." Ten years after the original track, with the complicity of Tony Williams, Herbie Hancock, and Ron Carter, Miles does nothing less than double the original tempo! Monk? Never! He sculpts in marble. Sometimes he touches up his tunes along the way. Like when he drops two bars from the bridge of "Criss Cross," or changes the rhythmic color of "Bye-Ya," but these are just details. Nothing really serious, for the basic material remains the same—marble. Monk makes mineral music. And you could feel this from the start in a radiant way. The year 1947 wasn't a loss at all; and it was the year he married Nellie, too. This was a fine beginning.

As his albums were not stirring up enthusiasm or break-ing any sales records, Monk kept on playing the clubs. Four years passed and he was leaving his mark here and there, but nothing truly glorious happened. He played a little in all the clubs, but rarely under his own name, and when he did, the place usually emptied out. Birdland, the Royal Roost, and the rest—places where his col-leagues triumphed, he was just content to play there, and pick up his pay. The club owners didn't care for him particularly, with his sly way of saying nothing but seeing right through them. To them, he was someone who was often late, didn't have a positive profile, and couldn't draw a crowd.

It's interesting to note that the musical debuts of his brilliant colleagues—Miles, Bird, Dizzy, Blakey and so many others—stood out immediately. These musicians did everything they could to carve a place for themselves: they went to New York and played with the best-known bands, using them as a springboard to the future they impatiently awaited. They hung out together. They put down the critics. They got talked about. They made a lot of noise. The jazz historian's job is made easier. You can see right away where they were playing, what they were doing and where they were going. But in Monk's case, it is completely different. During that period, it's difficult to track him down. For some strange reason, he remained in a mysterious shadow.

And yet, on studio dates, he was always in impeccable form. It makes you wonder what people back then had in their ears. His own recordings continued to cut vast new highways into virgin territory which he drove down with all the unerring vigor of genius. And he was accompanied by the most talented musicians in jazz: Milt Jackson, Sahib Shihab, Kenny Dorham, Lou Donaldson, Lucky Thompson, Shadow Wilson, Al McKibbon, Art Blakey and Max Roach—What a lineup!

And when he was invited to join the famous Verve session (*Bird and Diz*, 1950) to accompany the "inventors of bebop," he did his job with exemplary authority. His solos are cutting and brilliant; and his accompanying is flawless. From what you could see, he was finally ready for the gates of glory to open up for him. His playing is tight, and unwavering. His density, depth, precision, and originality are just begging for immediate recogniton. But it wasn't happening: As Bird and Diz are flying ever higher to glory, Monk seems to be spinning his wheels, like some kind of extra on the bebop stage. The guy you always see in the background, in all the scenes, who finally just seems to get in the way. You mind moving over, man, I'm trying to get a look at Bird. . . .

The cover photo on that Verve album shows Bird and Diz all smiles, as if beatified by their overwhelming success. But what you don't realize is that the photo has been cut! I saw the original, and on the right, just where it was cut, there is somebody else, and that somebody is Monk! Then it all becomes clear—one slash of the scissors, and you are rid of the party-crasher. Thanks, see you later! And yet, in that shot, just as on the record, Thelonious is perfectly in place. And the other two know it! You can see and feel it! They're all in it together!

But Monk's hour was yet to come. Just when Bird was harvesting the ripened fruit of his genius, Monk was still planting seeds in his private garden. And his family was starting to grow—in December 1949, Nellie gave birth to a son, and then, in 1953, to a daughter. Looking to the future, Thelonious must have had his eyes fixed on the Master Clock, which seemed to be telling him, Have patience, son, your hour will come.

But for the time being, his Blue Note experience hadn't been a financial success. Even so, he could feel that the people in the business were truly enthusiastic about his music. The Lions' place wasn't a factory. It was more like a workshop, run by bosses who had faith and passion. As we saw, he recorded a great deal with them. Anything more would have been either madness or patronage. So he cut his last tracks with them on May 30, 1952. And on October 15 of that year, he turned up at Prestige.

And there, things were cooking. The Prestige label had only been in existence for three years but it had already logged eighty-two recording sessions before Thelonious arrived! Bob Weinstock, the founder of the company, had gotten his recording experience working for Ross Russell at Dial Records, during the Charlie Parker sessions. But he was primarily known for his famous record store on 47th Street, the Jazz Record Center. He would place loudspeakers outside the store and play music all day long. There was no better place in town if you were interested in jazz, for it was located in the heart of the Broadway theater district, a few feet away from the Royal Roost, where Charlie Parker regularly appeared.

Just a few blocks uptown was 52nd Street, known as "Swing Street," where the jazz lover's wildest dreams came true. Also nearby was the Manhattan School of Music which more and more supplied talent to the ranks of bebop. They were the ones who filled the store. Weinstock's personal taste ran to the traditional, but he was open-minded, and they kept him up on the latest styles. "Why don't you start producing jazz records?" they'd ask him. "There's this cat named Tony Fruscella who can really blow—we know you'll dig him." Weinstock went to hear him and figured, Why not? He began to talk it over with Fruscella, but the trumpet player seemed hesitant, and kept talking about this monster alto player named Lee Konitz he wanted to introduce him to. Weinstock then went to Konitz who also backed down and suggested a friend of his named Lennie Tristano. Weinstock already knew about Tristano, who had records out, and good ones, too. So he decided to go with Lennie, and after they came to terms, the first record on the New Jazz label, the Lennie Tristano Quintet, came out on January 11, 1949, featuring Lee Konitz, but not Fruscella.

By late 1949, the New Jazz label was on the rise. It had already recorded Fats Navarro, Wardell Gray, Kai Winding, Terry Gibbs, Stan Getz, J.J. Johnson, Sonny Stitt, and others. The house drummers included Max Roach and Roy Haynes. And thirteen recording sessions had taken place during the year. New Jazz was just about to sign a distribution agreement with the label run by

Duke Ellington's son, Mercer Records, and the owner of Birdland was courting New Jazz to do the promotion for his new club.

Stimulated by his success, Bob Weinstock started recording artists of a higher market value, like Bud Powell. But he had to sell these records at a higher price, since the production costs were greater. Weinstock had to found a more exclusive label to illustrate the difference. And that is how the distinctive "Prestige" label was created.

The idea of two labels at the beginning, New Jazz and Prestige, had both advantages and drawbacks. It meant a larger organization to run, but it also provided the opportunity for trying artists out before launching them on the more prestigious recordings. This was the case for Max Roach, J.J. Johnson, John Lewis, and the young Sonny Rollins, who all began on New Jazz, and then wound up on Prestige. In the end, however, New Jazz was gradually absorbed by its younger brother Prestige, which then took over the entire catalog.

Weinstock's policy was to record, which was just what the musicians wanted. They were hoping, too, that there would be plenty of money in it, but that's another story. In any case, the bebop revolution, much of it recorded on Prestige, was like a tidal wave of energy and invention which broke over the world of jazz. The 1950's saw the birth of all kinds of schools—"cool jazz," "hard bop," "third stream," "West Coast," without even mentioning certain powerful personalities who can't be reduced to a school or a current, such as Rollins or Mingus. These musicians had to be recorded, and a great number of them came to Prestige.

Bob Weinstock's genius lay in signing up a number of artists with very different styles, first white, then black—

musicians who were as yet too young to be of interest to a major label. It was a radical choice, as it was about new music, and therefore a risky commercial decision. Prestige was a major change for Monk, for he was leaving a label where he was greatly admired, with the only challenge to his star status coming from musicians of a previous generation, like Sidney Bechet. Now he was becoming part of a company in which he did not have a monopoly on modernity and where he wasn't the only avant-gardist.

For Prestige already had the formidable Lenny Tristano, the innovative, groundbreaking pianist. He was a teacher, a *maître à penser*, and a tyrant. It is difficult to imagine that he didn't have a strong influence on Weinstock's artistic choices, at least at the beginning of the New Jazz adventure. Tristano had very fixed ideas on everything. He had students, or rather disciples, who were devoted body and soul. He even had a psychoanalyst brother to whom he'd send his problem students. He talked all the time about Charlie Parker or Bud Powell with the greatest admiration, but he consistently ignored Monk who was too remote from his own melodic and technical preoccupations.

And then there was Miles, who had left Capitol to join the ranks of the Prestige artists. He was only twenty-five but you could tell he had great promise. And, as he appealed to women, there was no doubt he would be a star. And there was Bud, who recorded with Sonny Stitt in January of 1950. Bud was Monk's protégé, his own personal discovery, and as he was considered bebop's most important piano player, it was hard to split the bill with him. The horn players consisted of the energetic Gene Ammons, the impressive Stan Getz, the most serious Lee Konitz, the smooth J. J. Johnson, the little known Wardell Gray, the young Sonny Rollins, and Monk's old sidekick Dizzy Gillespie.

When he came to Prestige, Monk had plenty of company, both friends and acquaintances. Some of them were selling well, and Thelonious hoped to gain rapid and lucrative recognition. Then Nelllie could quit her jobs, stay home with the kids and enjoy life a little. In a two-year period, Monk recorded seven sessions for Prestige, two of which were as accompanist for Miles and Rollins. It was a lot, for there was enough material in the five other sessions for almost four $33^1/3$ rpm. records of his own. One record every six months wasn't too bad!

Thelonious delivered brand-new material which was truly amazing. Fifteen new compositions, all masterpieces—I can't resist listing them: "Little Rootie Tootie," "Bye-Ya," "Monk's Dream," "Trinkle Tinkle," "Bemsha Swing," "Reflections," "Let's Call This," "Think of One," "Friday the 13th," "We See," "Hackensack," "Locomotive," "Work," "Nutty," and "Blue Monk." Enough! Somebody stop him! Trio, quintet, or quartet (under Rollins's name)—it's all good, and all new! And it has only been four months since he left Blue Note! How did he do it? He must have been stashing this stuff away! And what about the standards he picked out: "Sweet and Lovely," "These Foolish Things," and finally "Just a Gigolo," the first of a long series of solo versions which lasted right up to his final concert in 1976. This tune followed him throughout his career, like a mascot, and this was the first time he recorded it.

And there was also "Smoke Gets in Your Eyes," one of the loveliest melodies imaginable, by the brilliant composer Jerome Kern (who also wrote "Yesterdays," another of my favorites). Here it was arranged for quintet in the most disconcerting but still traditional way possible.

It would drive an arrangement teacher crazy, for it doesn't "sound" on paper, and yet it has an absolutely authentic flavor, as if Monk had written it himself. He certainly knew how to pick standards, and always had something to say on those tunes. And I'd bet my life he also knew the words. Max Roach recalled that he even put words to his own compositions; unfortunately, the only ones he could remember were to "Monk's Mood," which began, "Why do you evade facts?"—a very good question.

As for the original compositions, there are several which he rerecorded subsequently, including "Little Rootie Tootie," "Trinkle Tinkle," "Bemsha Swing," "Hackensack," and "Nutty." "Blue Monk," his big hit and what he considered his favorite tune, belongs to this period. (It's strange how composers are often most fond of their simplest inventions. Herbie Hancock's is "Maiden Voyage," which is based on an idea just as basic. Maybe it's because simple ideas allow for infinite variations.) Art Blakey, the indispensable brother, is on drums most of the time. Otherwise it's Max Roach, Art Taylor, Kenny Clarke, or Willie Jones, all first rate musicians. On bass, there's either Gary Mapp, Percy Heath, Curly Russell or Tommy Potter—always the perfect rhythm section. On horn, there's the superb Rollins, or else Frank Foster, who shows a total mastery of the understatements and difficulties of Monk's music. And then there is Miles for the famous session of Christmas 1954.

Here were some masterfully intelligent productions. Bravo, Mr. Weinstock, even if you were not the one who chose the musicians. You deserve a statue just for bequeathing this music to posterity.

What we can hear on Prestige in the course of those two brief years is the most independent, most agile, wild and compact Monk of his whole recording career. His fusion with Blakey is total. The compositions are all modern, swinging and definitive. Everybody felt like playing them. The solos are inspired and razor-sharp. It was still the days of three-minute cuts, and in a lifetime it would be hard to find three minutes as jam-packed and relaxed as these. The first chord of "Little Rootie Tootie," repeated nine times like a harsh manifesto, deserves a prize of its own. This tune was written for his son who had learned to whistle even before he could speak. Monk nicknamed him Tootie because of a cartoon of the time called "Little Toot the Talkboat," and the tune simply reproduces, in Monk's own way, the boat's joyous whistle. And on top of that, the quality of sound wasn't a mere detail. In fact, these Prestige recordings, along with four other records produced later (*Plays Duke Ellington, Nica's Tempo, The Unique,* and *Sonny Rollins, Vol. 2*), shared the privilege of being associated with Rudy Van Gelder, one of the greatest sound engineers the world has ever known.

We've talked about producers, but let's not forget the sound engineers. Sound is everything. Even though the persuasive power of Monk's music transcends the technical conditions of recording, his spirit and style were never more present than here. And that is thanks to Rudy's magic touch.

Van Gelder began in his own living room with nothing more than a Steinway piano (which Hank Jones considers the best piano he ever played), a few microphones and a mixing table. He lived in Hackensack, New Jersey, which gave its name to one of Monk's tunes. Later he moved to Englewood, where he is today, and the entire jazz world has filed through his studio. He is grouchy, tyrannical (no one's allowed to eat, smoke, or drink while recording is in progress), and as meticulous as an officer in white gloves. For more than thirty years, this passionate connoisseur has been leaving his imprint, crafting jazz music with his impeccable taste. In the 1980s, the "jazz sound" would take on a cleaner, subtler, more ethereal color, as on the records of the famous Manfred Eicher and his ECM label. But in the fifties, it was Van Gelder who set the standards of excellence. He was the man at Blue Note (unfortunately after Monk had already left). He was the man at Prestige. Savoy? That's him, too! The round presence of the piano, the definition of the drums, the rich depth of the bass, the warmth of the horns, that intelligent rapport between the instruments, where each musician finds his rightful place—all of that is Rudy! Monk meets Van Gelder! Hurray!

When the sound is good, any musician takes wing. Everything you play sounds good, your ideas flow, you feel like you're high. Each note effortlessly finds its exact place, and leaves the space around it open to the rest of the music. You can breath freely in the open space, and there is plenty of room. When the sound is bad, it's like ten people in a two-room apartment with the TV blaring. A good sound is a six-hundred-square-foot penthouse with a view of the Manhattan skyline.

This had to affect Monk. Rudy Van Gelder, the very master of sound. To understand the importance of sound, just take Thelonious's Blue Note albums. They have now been reissued on three compact discs entitled *The Genius of Modern Music*, volumes 1 and 2, and a third one under the name of Milt Jackson. The first two give a vision of Monk as hurried, unpredictable, and striking. But they don't do justice to his amazing mastery of space. The drums sound blurred and noisy, and the bass seems muffled. The horns sound good, but these are supposed to be a piano player's records, right? But then when you listen to the quartet with Milt Jackson (recorded by another sound engineer, by the way), you can hear everything.

Because recording the sound of a vibraphone is tricky. The amplitude cycles of the vibraphone are deep, and you have to record at low level, otherwise the sounds are quickly saturated. So even when the vibraphone is soloing, it sort of slips behind the sound of the piano, which can be recorded much closer. Here, Monk can play very little; he can let the notes die out, without having a cymbal crash end them prematurely. He can cultivate silence, without giving the impression of an absence. You can hear him there even when he isn't playing. His accompaniment to "Misterioso" is perfect in its economy and spontaneity. And that accompaniment is made possible by the sound, which generates, honors, and justifies it.

So, when Monk signed with Prestige, he was sure of getting true expertise which could only embellish his music. This was a definite consolation in a rather grim period, for he was no longer allowed to play publicly in New York. (Monk, the ultimate New Yorker!) He was making no money from gigs, his records weren't really selling, he had one child and another on the way, bills to pay, and, in 1953, his beloved mother Barbara died. And there were the first symptoms of serious psychological problems. The early fifties did not bode well.

Furthermore, his relations with Bob Weinstock were beginning to deteriorate. Weinstock seemed to prefer the young Miles Davis. And then there was the Modern Jazz Quartet which came on the scene in late '54, promising great things for a well-advised producer. Monk was not a priority, and that annoyed him. He also suspected Weinstock of not paying him the money he deserved. The American system can be quite vicious, and basically benefits the employer more than the employee. When you signed with a label, in a sense they "bought" you. A flat rate was agreed upon between the artist and the producer when the contract was signed, and which represented an advance on royalties. The record company reimbursed itself from the sales, and completed its payments when the royalties went over the original amount.

But in most cases, musicians never saw any of this remainder. Unless their music reached the Top 40, and they had financial clout, they never got to see the account books. And when you're black, barred from performing due to a drug offense, and broke as well, just go and try to sue a white man who is contributing to the American economy! Because of these flagrant injustices, in the late fifties various musicians including Gigi Gryce, Charlie Mingus and Ahmad Jamal started taking fate in their own hands and became their own producers and publishers. The establishment took a dim view of this: Downright Communists! I must be dreaming! Black people doing business!? At the time, this was a critical, but losing battle, for you needed vast amounts of energy, time, and money to bring about change. With the odds against you and all kinds of pressure being used, you quickly got sidetracked from your initial demand, which was simply to get the money they owed you. Before you knew it, you were defending the black cause, getting political, and your troubles were only beginning. And trouble wasn't really Monk's cup of tea. He had enough as it was. So he did what he always did—he kept his mouth shut and moved on along.

‖ 6 ‖

Piano Solo

At this time in Monk's life an event took place which was to have prophetic importance, its real significance only becoming clear much later. Monk made a trip to Paris. This was the first time he had been out of the United States and, though he didn't realize it then, it would be the chance to make his first solo record. This record was the cornerstone of one of the finest buildings in the history of jazz. And its story is well worth telling.

In the winter of 1953–54, Henri Renaud, a pianist and composer of the first generation of French boppers, went to New York to make a recording, and happened to meet up with Monk. It was a shock. Here he had simply come as a disciple to check out the Young Turks and he ran into the Grand Caliph himself. Monk responded sociably, received Renaud at home and the two soon became friends. As Renaud tells it, one night, a more philosophical one than others, they were sitting by the East River which, a few miles away, empties into the Atlantic. I wonder, Monk reflected, what it's like on the other side of the ocean. . . . Renaud had already learned that Monk never made pointless statements or asked empty questions, so he told him that there might be a way to show him at least a part of that other side, namely France.

After a quick call to Charles Delaunay in Paris who was putting the finishing touches on the 1954 Salon du Jazz, things became clearer. There wasn't enough money left to hire Monk for the Salon, Delaunay said, but it would be foolish not to have him come, so bring him over and we'll find him some work. So in June Monk landed in Paris to check it out. And in return, Paris got to check him out. In my opinion, this was more than a fair exchange.

That year, the big American star was not Thelonious. Except for a few well-informed jazzs fans, France did not care about him. Rather, it was Gerry Mulligan and his quartet which, ironically, was without piano. Paris was ready and willing to do anything for the playboy with the baritone. Another irony is that Monk and Mulligan became good friends shortly after that, and even recorded together (*Monk Meets Mulligan*, Riverside, 1957). And Gerry long remembered the admiration he had at the time for the brilliant composer of "Round Midnight."

The trip to Paris was certainly a tough lesson for Thelonious who was already well aware that no one is a prophet in his own country. But he realized he was even less so abroad. As he had come over alone, he had to use a local drummer and bass player to accompany him. Despite their efforts, they could not come near the energy or style of Art Blakey, or Curly Russell which complemented Monk so well. And in Paris he got more boos than applause. His only consolation was to meet a strange and impassioned woman who said she had flown over from London to hear him, and claimed to be Baroness Pannonica de Koenigswarter.

But what a trip! Who knows? This may have been the first time in his life he got booed like that. He wasn't like Miles the dandy, the lady-killer; or Bird, the genius, who left a host of awestruck, misty-eyed fans in his wake. No, in Paris Monk met with a skeptical incredulity, like an echo of his rejection by the New York public. We seemed to say, we don't need this stuff here!

We did the same thing to Coltrane. We were lucky they both came back. When they became famous, I wouldn't have blamed them if they'd told their producer, "If you don't mind, man, I'd rather not play in Paris. They're a sad bunch over there." But that wasn't the case, for the quality of determined people is that they don't bear a grudge, they overcome their rancor and they aren't affected by petty gibes. I'll never forget what Coltrane said just after the astounding concert he gave with his new group at the Olympia theater: "They're booing me because I'm not modern enough."

Fortunately there were a few Parisians in the know who took the trouble to record just over a half hour of what is, in my opinion, one of the most beautiful contributions to the music of the twentieth century. The piano was mediocre, which only made Monk's music all the more admirable. In solo, his face to the wind, Thelonious played eight of his compositions, and one standard, "Smoke Gets in Your Eyes," which he had just recorded for Prestige. All were played with a blend of determination and aplomb. He was confident and disarming, and that's why I love to hear him playing piano solo. In that basic form, freed of baggage and uncluttered, you can intimately savor his genius.

One of my favorite pieces is "Evidence." Here is its story. "Just You, Just Me" is a song Monk often enjoyed playing and one he recorded a few years later for Riverside in an updated and recast form with a memorable arrangement. As the starting point for this tune, Monk superimposed an eerie accompaniment on the basic chord structure which turned the usual order around: that accompaniment, with its personal accents, then becomes the melody. This is the sign of an exceptional composer: he inverts the standard order, and lifts the harmony and rhythm to a dominant melodic role. Simple and ingenious, this is the Monk trademark.

The first known version of "Evidence" is featured on the Blue Note album with Milt Jackson recorded in 1948, another monument of modern jazz, which I mentioned earlier. The first version of this young theme is made up of a dense eight-bar introduction, followed by a lean and cutting theme and accompaniment, softened by the agile vibraphonist's nonchalant ease. Then this composition lay dormant for six years, almost to the day.

When it surfaced again on the Parisian recording, the theme had taken on its definitive form. Monk used the most striking qualities of his 1948 sketch to create a finished work. And don't forget that "Evidence" is a double paraphrase: a melodic one, for it substitutes chords for the well-known theme of "Just You, Just Me," and a rhythmic one, in that the accents were carefully shifted, as opposed to a standard accompaniment. If you separate the piano from the bass and drums, you come up with something which is both rhythmically and melodically incomprehensible. Even the title, with its juvenile humor, is an example of this hermeticism: If there's just you, just me, there's just us, I mean justice! And for there to be justice there must be evidence, right? By its gradual shift in meaning, this pun perfectly fits Monk's musical ideas as he conceived this piece, and then took it several degrees beyond the fringe.

In that Parisian studio, Monk set out to play something which couldn't be taken at face value. For the tune to make sense, the rest of the rhythm section should logically be expected to maintain the basic framework on which Monk's clever structure has been superimposed. This was the chance for Thelonious to clearly demonstrate how he could become *his own rhythm section*. He doesn't play stride, but rather pushes three, and sometimes four voicings ahead at the same time, each one alternately expressing a fraction of the whole. It's like playing chess in 3-D! Or trying to herd fleas together. To play it, you have to exert absolute mastery over the tempo, harmony and melody all at once! In a different but comparable register, this technique takes place in Bach's celebrated *Goldberg* Variations in which four voices are simultaneously developed by only two hands. It's a bitch to play. Each finger follows its own particular idea without paying any attention to the others, and lays out when needed. Except that in Bach's time, there weren't any drums. And in the recording of "Evidence" you can sense them, even feel their presence.

Like a pole-vaulter who, in a single leap, breaks the world record by three feet, Monk, in half an hour, three thousand miles from home, for a radio program which he didn't know would become a record, set a new standard for the piano solo.

That day he invented an entirely new rhythmic density. No one had ever played solo piano like that before.

It was brand-new. This is the perfect record for a drummer who wants to practice a simple accompaniment rhythm. Crazy stuff is flying all over the place, but the tempo doesn't budge a fraction of an inch. It gives the impression of sound in total disorder, though perfectly organized—Thelonious, or the Art of the Free Fall. His way of seeming to fall, then catching himself, creates an unclassifiable and uncanny geometrical form. He is totally inpredictable. As he never balks, he's at the edge of catastrophe at every second, and takes risks that are completely forbidden for the standards of the time.

He is intimately familiar with flamboyant disaster. His tunes are torn apart every night, for how many people in New York can play his music correctly? But it doesn't matter to him—what counts is just moving ahead. And when he is at the piano by himself, with nobody to get in his way, Monk is right at home, in full confidence. He pushes his music ahead with power, candor, and depth, and invents a world of his own.

Since the subject has come up, I might as well address it right away: Did Monk have "technique"? Actually, even asking such a question reveals a desperate but undeniable fact: of all the types of artistic analysis, musicology is by far the most reactionary and obtuse. Does anyone ever question the "technique" of Douanier Rousseau? Or of Paul Klee, or Martha Graham, Céline, or Thomas Bernard? What is spontaneously accepted in all the other arts as the expression of an original voice making use of new techniques becomes immediately suspect in the world of music. You have to prove yourself, by belonging to a certain school, flashing your instrumental expertise, and by constantly referring back and prolonging tradition. The Franz Liszt syndrome. The quarrel between the Ancients and the Moderns, which was played out in literature and all the other arts ages ago, is still anchored firmly in musical minds. At the Sorbonne, only very recently have courses in jazz been made obligatory in order to obtain a degree in musicology. But what literature department ever dared grant a diploma which didn't take Ezra Pound or James Joyce into account? It's only normal that our American educational counterparts took less time than we did to institute jazz in the music curriculum. They were the first to raise this music from its status of folklore to that of universal art. But it's annoying to notice that within the world of jazz, the old quarrel still goes on in the same way.

And Monk paid the heavy price. He was thirty years old when he made his first record. In jazz (the same as in sports) normally by the age of thirty it's all over. You don't renew your items; rather, you sell from your stockroom, you settle down and open a store. But not Monk. For him, it was the beginning of his career. His musical concepts had been fully developed, but they came up against the opinion generally accepted by a majority of "connoisseurs": he didn't know how to play the piano.

When they began, the boppers met with a firm resistance to their music, which had broken sharply with tradition. But they'd never been accused of not knowing how to play their instruments. They even proudly acknowledged the influence of their idols in the previous generation—Lester Young for Bird, or Roy Eldridge for Dizzy. But Monk never acknowledged anyone. Whenever someone insisted on the question of his influences, particularly that of Duke Ellington, he made it a point of honor to avoid the question, or else replied that in all honesty, his only inspiration was himself.

But you can be sure that he knew how to play piano. Many of his characteristic traits are veritable technical puzzles. He must have spent entire days on each of them. The rhythmic precision, the importance of accents, the hand independence, and the control of time, were all mastered with royal authority, and were the product of hours of work. That kind of technique does not come by itself—you have to work at it. At home, Monk could play the same tune for hours, polishing it up and squeezing every bit of juice from it. So when he hit the bandstand, he was as ready as anyone could ever be. As pianist Barry Harris said, "At home, the other musicians practiced their instruments; but Monk practiced music." And not just any kind, for it was *his* music. It was the piano, of course, but totally in the service of his idea of jazz. In these conditions, it's not surprising that, in the beginning, he found so few ears to listen to him. Without the reassuring world of references, it's hard to judge anything.

And yet, his music doesn't present any revolution in *form*. In fact, looking over the whole of his work, I was amazed to see a total scorn for form, contrary to what I had first believed. What do I mean by form? Quite simply, the structure which organizes a piece of music from the first note to the last. It's an old subject in all the arts, but particularly in music where the principle of repetition is practically inevitable. One of the composer's prime preoccupations concerns the organization of this repetition, as well as the variations connected with it. The "format" of the small bebop groups is based on a simple rule: a theme, or head played once or twice (usually with a bridge, like A-A-B-A), an improvisation on the tune structure, then the melody one last time. Once that norm was accepted, it wasn't long before the artists a few years younger than the inventors of bebop started shaking it up, enlarging or refining it. Even in his early Prestige years, Miles showed a pronounced taste for subtle and original structuring which would give new youth to the melodies he was recording. John Lewis, with the Modern Jazz Quartet, turned to the structures of classical music in order to extend the principle of improvisation. The list is endless, and attains the very explosion of form with the pioneers of free jazz, such as Ornette Coleman and Cecil Taylor.

But for Monk, the problem never arises. Form is a kind of basic necessity, since each music has one, but does not deserve any particular attention. The case of "Evidence" is a perfect example: it imposes a clever and original conception *within* a given form, without challenging the principle of the form. Also, Monk used perfectly standard structures in his compositions, of twelve, sixteen, twenty-four, or thirty-two bars; but suddenly he would decide that no one would ever take a solo on "Crepuscule with Nellie." Or, for "Coming on the Hudson," he would write a five-bar melody, with a three-and-a-half-bar bridge. This being said, when you compare it to the composition "Four in One," for example, just try and recognize the very ordinary chord progression behind it, which also served as the basis for twenty other melodies! Even in a basic blues like "Straight, No Chaser," you get turned around!

I always loved the way Thelonious referred to the bridge of a song. Americans have a dozen or so names for this almost obligatory passage in all melodies: the bridge, the channel, the tunnel, et cetera. But Monk called it "the inside." What mattered was the heart of the music, and to get as close as possible to it. Thelonious used the standard forms of his day like empty shells which his genius would inhabit. And if the melody happened to be five bars long, that's just too bad—you had to improvise on five bars. Thelonious always built tunes he felt at home in. If the angles were all of a sudden too tight or narrow, he just pushed them out.

Same thing for the order of solos. Each musician played on the changes, then passed it on to the next when he was through. This is a far cry from the lengthy suites of Bud Powell, such as "The Glass Enclosure," in which he carefully combines unisons, ostinatos, and improvisations in an obvious concern for form. Despite the rare exception, this was much simpler with Monk, with just melody, solos, and melody. His music didn't suffer in the least, and its modernity exists at a completely different level. He doesn't relate to the current history of jazz, and he doesn't constantly try to push the accepted limits of form like his contemporaries did. For what he is interested in, more than form, is the content.

Actually, the modernity of Monk's compositions was not exactly unique, and it is easy to forget that similar colors were used with just as much audacity by at least two of his friends and contemporaries, Elmo Hope and Herbie Nichols. These two fine pianists shared along with Bud Powell a great admiration for Monk. Elmo Hope was six years younger than Thelonious (and a year older than Bud), at a time when a few years was enough to create a generation gap, as history was moving rapidly. When Johnny Griffin met Thelonious in New York in 1948, he said Monk was always with Bud and Elmo. This turned-on trio cruised the city day and night looking for pianos to play. Elmo and Bud would compete playing Bach's Inventions; then they'd duel it out with Monk's compositions, under the benevolent and sarcastic eye of the master himself. As for Herbie Nichols, it was surely no accident that he, too, had a solid classical training, which paradoxically led him to play more Dixieland than either bebop or his own music. And when he recorded under his own name, on Savoy (1952) or Blue Note (1955–56), it was with Monk's usual accompanists: Shadow Wilson, Al McKibbon, Art Blakey, or Max Roach.

Elmo Hope and Herbie Nichols were two remarkable pianists and composers who remained in Monk's shadow. Yet they shared with him the same melodic sense, and the same originality. Why were they forgotten? Because their personalities were less extravagant, or their lucky star was dimmer? Or was it because they had a more conventional technique and velocity? The picture without the sound?

In his improvisations, Monk offers a totally original phrasing and accentuation. Where Nichols and Hope play their own works with a traditional technique, Monk mixes his technique with his music and presents an inalienable whole of incredible aesthetic power. And it was the same Herbie Nichols who praised Monk in a *Music Dial* magazine article in 1946: "When Monk takes a solo, he seems to be partial to certain limited harmonies which prevent him from taking his place beside Art Tatum and Teddy Wilson. He seems to be in a vice as far as that goes and never shows any signs of being able to extricate himself." What an admission of helplessness— and what an unexpected definition of schizophrenia!

Monk's music can neither be classified nor assimilated. Not because it is revolutionary, which isn't a reason in itself, but because it's like a rock thrown into a pond which immediately sinks and disappears. You watch it going down, and you don't know whether to keep your eye on the sinking mass, or to contemplate the concentric ripples of the tremors. There's nothing in Monk's "style" for a pianist: there's nothing you can steal, and practice in the twelve keys, then use it on the gig to sound hipper than hip.

And when you try it, it just gets in the way, sticking out like a sore thumb. And why wouldn't it get in the way? Fifty years ago it was already in the way, and it took all the obstinacy, humor and patience of Monk to get it accepted. And neither criticism nor history know where to put it, for it seems disorderly. You can't digest a rock or a stone. There is no affiliation, no august and venerable school, no heirs, no spiritual fathers, disciples or students. Mother and father unknown. No descendants. So it takes time to acknowledge the fact that this even exists.

People tried to connect him with Duke Ellington, or with James P. Johnson; and Randy Weston and Abdullah Ibrahim claim that Monk greatly influenced them. That's all true, but after all, the only chance for a musician to connect himself to Monk is to start thinking along the same lines. Which is a particularly delicate exercise. You can't simply flatten the fifth instead of augmenting it. You have to wonder just what a piano really is, or a rhythm section, a solo, an accompaniment, or a melody.

Bebop brought in a vast number of new chords, harmonic audacity, and chord substitutions. But it was sixteenth notes for everybody—no favorites. As if what a pianist played was the same as a trumpet player or saxophonist. The phrasings of Bird and Bud set new standards. And too bad for those who had trouble with their instruments which weren't adapted to the new rules of velocity, like the trombone. Get to work, son; you can't leave your room till you sound like J. J. Johnson.

But Monk not only instigated this advanced harmonic

research, but also understood that he had to find a *sound*. Max Roach told how, by using that characteristic technique of hitting two notes a half tone apart then releasing one of them a fraction of a second later, Monk aimed at imitating the pitch-bend effect that a horn can have. A fascinating process, but it was doomed to failure. For, as the piano is a tempered instrument, it is impossible to alter the intervals on the keyboard. But at the end of this search, like a gold miner who happens to hit oil, Monk unearthed uncanny sound treasures! And he rapidly demonstrated that a certain chord or phrasing played on one octave of the piano wouldn't have the same sound one octave higher or lower. Stated like that, it sounds obvious, but such an approach entails a complete knowledge of the whole instrument, at a time when piano dexterity only gave a relatively minor importance to these highly musical resources. Monk always plays the combinations of notes *appropriate to the specific register of the instrument.*

Or he plays a conflicting chord and, after a couple of seconds, releases the clashing notes, thus bringing out, stark naked, a luminous chord. Just after they met, he and Mulligan played this game for days. The pianist also taught the science of maximum economy in the choice of the notes making up a chord. Why play three when two were enough? And that's another torture for whomever tries to reproduce Monk's music: you always think you're hearing more notes than he's actually playing. You always have to ask yourself, Is he really playing that, or do I just *think* he is? And that ruthless selection that Thelonious imposes on himself is based on a highly developed understanding of the world of overtones.

For those unfamiliar with this concept, one single note played on the piano contains an infinity of others, hidden behind it. In physics, this is quite clear: the note you hear in the foreground, which corresponds to a certain frequency, is at the same time accompanied, in a less audible way, by all its multiple frequencies, and so by all the corresponding notes, separated from the main note by an interval of an octave, then by a fifth, a third, et cetera. These are the overtones, which piano tuners use as points of reference when they tune a piano. They are also the high-pitched and crystalline notes you produce by picking a guitar string without pressing it all the way down to the neck. They are called "overtones," a good term, for the tones are superimposed.

One could even say that the sharpness of an ear can be measured by the ability to hear all these frequencies. Mastering this science is difficult, especially when applied to a whole chord and not just one note. Each note's overtone then becomes fused and produces a thick forest of conflicting frequencies, different each time depending on the chord that is played. And when you study Monk's work, you start to wonder if he didn't have a superhuman ear, the way he mastered the art of subtle understatement.

For here lies one of the most beautiful secrets of his music: how to make something sound without playing it. Trumpetist Eddie Henderson told of one night in San Francisco when he saw Thelonious drenched in sweat, touching the keys, but so smoothly that no sound came from the piano for a whole set. The logical conclusion! It's absurd, but perfectly logical! And this actual philosophy of understatement holds true, in all aspects of both his music and his life. That's how he raised the discipline of the piano solo to such dizzying heights. He can make you hear a bass, drums, a whole band, when he's just there alone with his instrument. But not in an exuberant manner, like the traditional virtuosos do. On the contrary, he does it with the most frugal economy. He turns his back on clichés, and by means of an incomprehensible magic, he expresses more with less. That's why you can perceive, with a fleeting and ever-changing feeling, the whole history of jazz in one single interpretation of his. And that's why, throughout his life, he kept his interest in seemingly insignificant details—things like a felt-tipped pen, or a street, or a ray of sunshine, or a button. Or a play on words like "Evidence," or "Little Rootie Tootie" and its cartoon introduction—it was all grist for his mill. Anyone who ever knew him was struck by his attention to trivial details, which he would comment on with disproportionate depth, the way a child would speak.

I have an entomologist friend who is the same way. He starts turning stones over in a field and within a few minutes uncovers a scorpion, three fly larvae, five beetles—a whole mass of insects, and evidence of a hidden world, as complex as our own. Thelonious is just like that. He can give voice to what is beneath the surface, hidden from the blasé ears and eyes of ordinary mortals. . . . He can say it all with just a few notes, a few signs, and you can imagine the discipline which that requires.

It all comes down to this unarguable truth: Monk has a *sound*. And it is so powerful, so imperious, that it fits all musical styles from standard or modern jazz to blues, ragtime, or bebop—Monk the unclassifiable! Same for the instruments—he can get a sound out of anything from a Steinway or a Baldwin to a beat-up old upright. As soon as he puts his fingers on the keyboard, it *sounds*. It's amazing how his music transcends the sad pianos (like the one on his famous Paris recording of 1954), the bad recordings (the first Blue Note sessions, at the dawn of modern sound engineering) and the lousy stereo systems (like mine). His sound is so strong that it cuts through matter with the hardness of a diamond. So many musicians feel completely helpless if they don't have the proper material conditions. Keith Jarrett sends a piano back if it's not on a par with his talent. Not Monk. It's not important—his music is above all that.

It's interesting to note that the two record companies that really believed in him, Blue Note and Riverside, had art directors whose tastes, up to then, ran more toward traditional jazz. The paradox is that while Monk was long ignored because of his extreme modern style, those who gave him his first try were impressed by his classicism. Which shows just how far his music is beyond fashion, currents or schools, how self-sufficient it is. On any instrument, in any circumstances, there are no limits! He did not care about the present, or its contingencies. Or else, he circumscribed the problem so definitively that it's been solved once and for all.

So Thelonious cut his first solo tracks in Paris. He was already thirty-six years old, and would have to wait another three years before his producer decided to accord the merited importance to the piano solo form. This first "official" solo recording (*Himself*, Riverside, 1957) was followed by a number of others. Without exception, right down to the last one he recorded in London in 1971, they all produced the same miracle: Monk held all music within his own two hands.

‖ 7 ‖

Producers II

The time has come to meet Orrin Keepnews. He and Monk had met each other in 1948 when Keepnews was a young journalist with *Record Changer* magazine and Monk had just finished his first Blue Note recordings. This wasn't the first time that the press was interested in him, but Monk remembered this interview as having been particularly insightful and intelligently done, and had kept a mental note of it for seven years. And then, in late 1954, rumor had it that Monk was fed up with Prestige and was ready to change companies. Keepnews, a longtime admirer, jumped at the chance and got in touch with Weinstock to find out if Monk was free of contract obligations. You can have him, Weinstock said, as long as he pays the $108.27 he owes me. (Here, now, the accounting gets precise.) What a bargain for Keepnews! And not a very good one for a thirty-seven-year-old pianist who, according to all his colleagues, is obviously a genius. One hundred eight dollars. Because of the irony of the price, as well as the joy of getting such a good deal, Keepnews framed a photostat of this famous check and hung it in his office.

For Monk, this was like starting all over again, and he was getting impatient. Riverside, the company of Keepnews and Bill Grauer, was a small, young label which only handled reissues of old classics by people such as Louis Armstrong, King Oliver, Ma Rainey, and Jelly Roll Morton. By all appearances, Keepnews was straight, well-informed, liberal, and even progressive in his understanding of jazz musicians' problems. And he was a writer, and made his opinions public and held definite views about jazz life, so at least it seemed like he could be trusted. But still, Monk was on his guard. Keepnews admitted that he never became close friends with Thelonious, despite their cordial and confident relationship. This was probably due to their respective personalities. Also, Thelonious had learned his lesson at Prestige, and had become particularly sensitive to the fact that producers made their money from his talent. He also saw that Keepnews had the pride and the ambition to become an intelligent producer, one who could boast of the influence he had over musicians. And Monk was not ready for that.

But Keepnews was right. In my opinion, he was the only producer in the whole of Monk's career who successfully played the part of a real artistic director. He didn't simply start the tape running, the way the people had done at Blue Note (with great pleasure), or at Prestige (carelessly). Rather, he tried to influence the course of Monk's artistic life, and had excellent ideas as a producer. And that was due to both ambition and inexperience. Ambition, for he understood the importance and the novelty of Monk's music, and saw the rut Monk was in. Orrin wanted to draw him out and let the whole world discover him in a new light. By inexperience, also, for he had never produced records and didn't know what he was getting into with Monk, who had never met anyone to tell him what he should record. Keepnews could have made a better choice to start with, but that's what I love about him. In a different way, he must have been as stubborn as Monk, and that deserves a prize in itself.

The first thing the producer had to change was the overall negative image of the high priest of bebop. Unfortunately developed by Alfred and Lorraine Lion, this representation of his music had followed him to Prestige, where nothing had been done to correct it. Monk was still considered an obscure, hermetic composer. That had to be remedied immediately. The producer's first idea was to have him play someone else's music. The second idea was to have him play only the music of Duke Ellington for his first record on Riverside. Very subtle! Keepnews couldn't have made a better choice. Although his popularity was in a slump (like the rest of jazz), and only started to pick up as of 1955–56, Duke Ellington was still the only black composer in the field of great American melodies to vie for first place with George Gershwin and Cole Porter. For "traditional" repertoire, there was no one better. This daring new production idea was one which the inspired Norman Granz had already tested with the Oscar Peterson Trio and the famous "songbooks" (an entire record devoted to the work of one composer) in late 1952. And it just so happened that the composers Granz used were Gershwin, Porter and—Ellington. This idea had been a commercial success, and I suppose that's why Keepnews decided to try it out with Monk. This was a radical change in the pianist's musical direction. Now he was moving toward more profitable ventures.

Choosing Duke as the Trojan horse with which to attack the Top 40 is a real stroke of genius. The lunar Monk meets the Ellington sun! The music speaks directly to Monk, and is part of his instinctive heritage. And he doesn't object to the production idea, for he can see that his musical convictions aren't compromised in the least. In fact, Monk slips on Duke's music like a custom-made glove, as usual. And instead of recording a copy version, he dresses the music up in the most amazing and personal garments one could imagine. Duke with a new look! updated! new wave! "I Got It Bad," a classic Ellington ballad, is transposed from its original tempo and played as a poignant, medium swing tune. "Black and Tan Fantasy" remains oblivious to the dramatic colors of the original version, and "It Don't Mean a Thing" is reduced to its simplest and most rhythmic form. "Sophisticated Lady," treated with juvenile nonchalance; and the popular melody "I Let a Song Go out of My Heart," played in the most classical trio style. "Solitude," in solo, naturally—with depth and determination. And in "Mood Indigo," the introduction alone expresses all the modernity and radicalism of Monk's interpretation.

It is hard to believe that Monk didn't write any of these compositions. But maybe there is something restrained or modest about this album which could give us a clue. It could be in the affectionate and sincere distance he takes towards the tunes. Or in the emphatic arpeggios which he rarely uses in other contexts. When Duke played these pieces, he didn't hesitate in the least to invest them with all his strength of aesthetic persuasion. He played them in depth. But Monk stays a little on the edge—as if he was just borrowing the tunes, not stealing them. He is happy and relaxed, and you can feel it. He made Duke's music shine in his own special way, with no affectation.

His fellow musicians are particularly well chosen: Oscar Pettiford, aside from the authenticity he brings to the repertoire (as a former member of the Ellington band), also plays with a passion and an expertise which are in perfect balance with the calm assurance of the masterful Kenny Clarke —who knows Monk inside out after all the years they have spent together at Minton's. The golden triangle. With sound engineer Rudy Van Gelder providing the jewel's setting, this is a flawless diamond of a session composed almost entirely of first takes—a producer's dream. My only regret is that the famous record cover, a reproduction of Douanier Rousseau's *The Lion's Feast* (What artistic intuition on the part of Keepnews! Not bad for a producer!), was used only when the album was reissued in 1958. When the record first came out, the cover featured a simple photo of the trio. Otherwise, it would have been perfection at the first shot, the ultimate state of grace.

Eight months later he does it again. This time Keepnews plays another trump card and asks Monk to record an album of standards. Monk responds with seven little gems of well-tempered modernism, rearranged with impeccable taste. Seven pieces serendipitously processed by the Monk-o-matic blender and served up brighter, fresher, and more appealing than ever. The same bass player is there, but Kenny Clarke has moved to Europe, and is replaced by Monk's old buddy Art Blakey. Thanks to Blakey, the session acquires a virulence which, in a certain mood, you could almost wish had been there on the earlier recording. The bear's paw has even more heft, as Monk kicks out the jams. On "Just You, Just Me," he smashes his long-distance record (not counting the memorable "Friday the 13th," recorded two years before) by running the tune to a breathtaking seven minutes fifty-eight seconds. You get the feeling that it is so good, he can't stop. The master of concision and the sworn enemy of the superfluous lets himself take a few more spins around the track. The rhythm section is in overdrive. The musicians possess every detail of the tune so thoroughly (remember its paraphrase, "Evidence"?), and the Van Gelder sound is so good, that it would be a crime not to take advantage of it. And he does. What a letdown when it stops! One more time! What a crew! Eight minutes! Give us ten, fifteen, fifty—who gives a damn, as long as it doesn't stop! It's just too good! Why stop? Not enough room on the record? Just put on another one!

The result? A total flop. The very people who reproached Monk for his obscurity wouldn't forgive this unacceptable compromise. That's how little they knew of Thelonious, who in musical terms didn't even know the meaning of the word *compromise*. But it didn't matter, for now the slate had been wiped clear, and all that would only be significant later. The quality and intuition of this production choice would dazzle Monk's detractors when the huge tidal wave of his popularity broke, once and for all, a year later. People had to admit that everything Monk touched turned to gold, even if they did so begrudgingly. Some people were a little slow on the uptake, but Monk was used to that. And as Keepnews was stubborn, it would eventually pay off. In life, you have to be persistent.

But then, one would ask, isn't Monk composing any more? Has the wellspring of those extraordinary, unpredictable melodies run dry? Has Thelonious run out of inspiration? That's impossible! It's not because his producer has decided to boost his image that he's given up. And since the Riverside people are telling him to take it easy for a while, well, he could just take his other compositions to the Signal record label. It's not healthy to keep it all for yourself. You have to let it out or you'll get sick. So between these two "standard" Riverside albums, he records more modern compositions with Gigi Gryce, whom he greatly admires (*Nica's Tempo*, 1955). "Shuffle Boil," "Brake's Sake," and "Gallop's Gallop"— damn! This is some solid stuff! And once again with Van Gelder doing the sound. These tunes are so outrageous, and so difficult, that he only pulled them out when he was at the top of his form, in 1964. It takes tenacity and daring to play them. These puzzles of high art are extremely sinuous, though limpid. And Gigi Gryce could play them with casual nonchalance: Monk's music hard to play? Are you kidding? These tunes are elementary — just play them the way they're written.

Which simply proves that Monk could roam the beaten paths of Riverside, but still wander off into his own haunts—strange, remarkable lands which bore the Monk signature . . . cutting swaths through forests which open on to vast, uncharted clearings . . . the elephant's burial ground . . . So many people would love to have a map to reach these virgin territories, but Monk's the only one who knows how to get there. You have to follow the guide. I can picture Monk as a sherpa, stepping across deep chasms on an unsteady bridge made of knotted vines. Monk's particular know-how is based on his attention to detail. It's all in how you knot the vine. And his vine bridges were built to last. He practices the mysterious science of improvising with bits and pieces of string, simple ideas and common sense. Everything in Monk's music has its own luminous importance—which is why it's so hard to avoid mysticism when talking about him. Later, you realize that this kind of wobbly balance, and resolute ignorance toward academicism which immediately strikes you on first listening to him, is the result of extreme concision and calculation. There is no user's guide to Thelonious Monk and his music. He's the only one who knows how to do it, and that's all there is to it.

When he recorded his third album, *Brilliant Corners*, on the Riverside label in 1956, this suddenly became obvious. Monk's hour had come at last. When the record was released in 1957, Monk was thirty-nine years old. Talk about wandering in the wilderness! He had already recorded twenty-two sessions, and seventeen of those were under his own name! The strangest thing of all is that he would find favor with both the critics and the public alike only when he stuck to his guns and maintained his most radical positions, despite all his producer's efforts to the contrary. And I believe that Monk developed most as a composer in this period of his life. Judge for yourself: He had been making records for almost ten years but had never once rehashed a musical idea—his compositions were constantly fresh and original. The Monk music machine was working overtime on three shifts! So you shouldn't be surprised if he pushed things a little farther out each time. But here he had gone beyond the fringe, beyond the famous critical point. And it just so happens that in this album he started looking back through his repertoire, and came up with "Bemsha Swing," recorded in the Prestige days. After that, his new compositions would appear less frequently, but were still as beautiful as ever.

The composition "Brilliant Corners," however, is truly something special. All standard jazz conventions are shattered. Monk has never before carried his utter comtempt for rules so far. The tempo is doubled, then cut several times in a row in the same tune. The effect is baffling, but the master remains in complete control. The "bridge" is written in seven bars, instead of the usual eight or sixteen. Nothing is square or symmetrical; it is all askew. Monk's own peculiar melody line rules supreme, and more than ever the solos are subordinated to it. With the possible exception of alto player Ernie Henry, the musicians on this session were the cream of the professional crop: Sonny Rollins, Max Roach, and Oscar Pettiford. But even they were sucking wind and wound up spending a whole night on this big keynote number without getting a complete version down. This forced Keepnews to perform an astute splicing operation so the session wouldn't be a total disaster.

"Brilliant Corners." The title alone sounds surrealistic. There had been plenty of weirdness already, like "Off Minor," "Epistrophy," or "Trinkle Tinkle," but now things were moving into another dimension! This being said, from a strictly formal point of view, the basic idea of the tune is again simple and brilliant. The band plays the head, but in unison—bass, drums, everybody. That may not sound so brilliant on the printed page but, to my knowledge, it had never been done before by a jazz quintet. And it provided one more scorching, brand-new sound. This tune belongs to the family of Monk's "*marches grotesques*," to which I would add "Friday the 13th," "Jackie-ing" or "Coming On the Hudson." And in unison, it pays off. Played in a slow tempo, you can't miss. It would be hard to highlight a melody more than this.

The second brilliant idea is this: As it's being played, turn the march into a "jazz tune," by doubling the tempo with the walking bass and the ride cymbal—now life swings as the Monk fountain of youth springs. The third brilliant idea is sticking to the first two ideas, while having the solos alternate between the slow and fast parts. The broken-record syndrome. The only problem comes when you try to cut it. Going from simple to double time is a cinch. But when, in an uptempo number, you have to put the brakes on coming down the hill and, in a single bar, get off your bike and start marching again, that's something else. It's not exactly what you'd call a natural movement. All mountain climbers know it well—going up is a lot easier than coming down. Then when you take a look at the chords you're supposed to solo on, things really get tough.

The idea itself is simple. Today, in 1997, the tune isn't all that tricky. By now we've seen a lot worse. But this was back in 1956 (October 15, to be exact—days like that tend to stand out). Keepnews confided that Monk left the session exasperated at being unable to find musicians who could play such an easy tune. Now, forty years later, you can understand him. But that just shows how ahead of his time he was. The work of a true pioneer, there was no conceivable equivalent to this tune until much later, from people like Charlie Mingus or Ornette Coleman. For it was based on musical ideas that were unheard-of at the time. This wasn't music, it was obstination. And that's the most brilliant thing. You can almost hear a voice in the background saying, "Give up, Thelonious, it'll never work!" But Monk followed his idea all the way through, and the result is amazing.

For you've got to be nuts to write a tune like that. Your self-confidence must be impermeable. Here, Rollins is at the rudder, in a sea of changing tempos; and the only bearings he can get for his solos are chords which aren't even related, coming either too slow or too fast.

Ernie Henry, terrified at the idea of missing the boat, stands staring at his watch. Max Roach just can't get used to the idea of a seven-bar bridge, and adds one more to his solo, like he knows what he's doing. And yet all three, just like Monk, are true New Yorkers. This is a family affair, and should make the music easier. And then there's Oscar Pettiford as trailblazer—the mixed-blood Oklahoma Indian, making signals for the other braves to get back in line. And the imperturbable Monk surges ahead with his usual assurance, giving the steering wheel a spin just when the whole madcap escapade is about to flip over! It's amazing there isn't a single fatality. One false move and it's curtains. There is no better example than this of what Coltrane said about Monk's music: "Miss one chord and you feel like you're falling down an elevator shaft." All the musicians at the session have their tires screeching, trying to make the hairpin turns at breakneck speed! The whole studio smells like burning rubber. Poor Orrin Keepnews must be tearing his hair out in the control room. Everything seemed to be going so smoothly. Systems break down! Red alert! We're going to crash! Why did I ever sign this guy? What am I doing still alive? His liner notes about the session in the Riverside collection begin with typical British aplomb: "In many ways, this marked the true beginning of my work with Monk." Whew, baby! "Work," did you say? More like what Hegel referred to as "work, patience, and negative agony." And, on top of it all, Monk and Pettiford got in an argument (they never played together again after this session)—what a mess! The very first night there, Monk found a celesta in a corner of the studio and insisted on using it for "Pannonica"! A couple of days later Max discovered some timpani drums and pounded them furiously throughout "Bemsha Swing!" What is this madhouse? You call this a jazz record?

And yet, the public made no mistake: In *Brilliant Corners*, they enthusiastically applauded the pianist's most radical stance. With his back to the wall, Monk pulled out his bag of tricks and turned the tables on everyone! Real suspense! Definitely a close call. If this didn't knock people out, you might as well throw in the towel. Too bad for them—we quit. The doomed artist dies in obscurity. Then a few years later his greatness is recognized. ("My God, we've burned a saint!"). But fortunately this time, the world woke up and Thelonious finally escaped the unjust fate that had been dogging him for years. The public can be pretty sadistic. They waited for Monk to raise the stakes as high as possible—and God knows they were already high—before finally declaring: "He's okay after all; let's keep him."

It may have been a coincidence, but just before recording this album, the apartment where Thelonious was living with his family went up in flames. In the disaster, he lost everything he owned, including the piano, sheet music, contracts, photos, records, and furniture. This isn't unusual in New York where the poor condition of the buildings (together with the criminal greed of the landlords) is a constant threat to the inhabitants. But when it happens to you, you see your whole life going up in smoke. This is a grim predicament when you think of all the energy it takes to acquire and maintain a litle piece of private property in New York City. And this is happening at the most critical moment of Monk's career. He has been recording for ten years but is still unknown and in financial straits, and there is nothing promising on the horizon. Then suddenly things are looking up, as if fate had demanded a tribute. Once the past is wiped out, you can start all over again on a new footing. In a sense, this was Monk's ritual fire sacrifice.

He immediately bought a new piano which was so long it encroached on the kitchen, and recorded his first solo album (*Himself*, 1957). At this time, he went back to his old habit of blending personal compositions with standards in the course of the same session. Once again, things were going smoothly. He got his cabaret card back. And then, in early summer, he got a gig at a small, little-known club on the Lower East Side called the Five Spot with his trio (soon to be a quartet) featuring Wilbur Ware, Shadow Wilson, and a new sensation by the name of John Coltrane.

The group was like a bombshell. The club was packed each night, and people were starting to say, How could we have ignored Monk for so long; this cat is great! Where has he been all this time? The band was hired to stay on— as long as people came to listen. Monk played there almost continuously for more than a year. The line of people waiting to get in went all the way around the block. Suddenly the whole town wanted to see him in action. In December of that year, Monk's New York success was broadcast nationwide when his trio was featured on the CBS television program *The Sound of Jazz* along with other jazz greats including Billie Holiday, Count Basie, Coleman Hawkins, and Ben Webster.

Monk was forty years old, and his hour had finally come. Now he had a chance to catch his breath and take a look back. Things were going well. First of all, he had found an agent, and agents are important because they find gigs, arrange contracts, and bring in work. Unless a jazz musician is well known, he usually handles his own business. For example, some club manager happens to hear a band playing in New York, and at the break says to the bandleader, "I've got a place down in Baltimore, you feel like coming down to play there next month?" When they agree on the money, the organizer sends the contract and the deal is concluded. It's the snowballing principle: The more you play, the more you're in demand, until the avalanche starts and the artist can't handle it all by himself. Then an agent usually steps in, offers his services and takes a cut of anywhere from ten to twenty percent of the musician's salary. That's in the best of cases. In the worst, there are no concerts, thus no need for an agent. In 1955, when Monk left Prestige, he didn't have many gigs. In a way, this was fortunate, as he wasn't of any financial interest to an agent who was looking to make money. If someone approched him, it was out of love for his music, and not for the profit. Besides, an agent can be a threat to a musician's career. As his main objective is to keep the money rolling in, he could place "his" artist in an inappropriate context. And in the case of Monk, this would have been a catastrophe. But on the other side, the enthusiastic fan is also a danger. Being unfamiliar with the way the business works, he might lead his protégé astray out of ignorance, whereas the real pro would do it out of greed. But Thelonious had flair. His finesse and psychological insight enabled him to recognize the rare gem when it appeared in the person of Harry Colomby.

He and Monk first spoke when Monk was playing in a club with Art Blakey. At the time, Harry was a highschool teacher, and a jazz fan, and had invited Blakey to play at his school. He went to the club to give Blakey directions to the school. Now, Harry just happened to have a brother named Jules who ran Signal Records, for whom Monk had recorded with Gigi Gryce only a few weeks before. So the first thing Harry said when he met Monk at the bar of the club was, "I'm Jules's brother." This was the perfect introduction, for that session had been pleasantly free of the usual recording pressures that Monk had been going through at the time. For Monk, the name Colomby meant things were Okay. He smiled: "Yeah, I remember; you live uptown, right? You got a car? You mind dropping me off?" (Harry didn't live uptown at all, but he admired Monk too much to let this chance go by.) "Sure," he said; "but let's make it quick; I have classes tomorrow and I have to get up at six." By the time he dropped Monk off at his doorstep, Harry had become his agent. During the ride uptown, Harry expressed his enthusiasm for Monk's music, and told him that his success depended only on his determination and his refusal to compromise. Thelonious liked what he heard, and a friendship began which lasted until Monk's death. (At this writing, Colomby is still alive.) That's the way Monk was—he did everything by feeling. And here he made no mistake, for Harry was the best and most honest agent he ever could have found. And for a musician, that is something precious.

By early 1958, Colomby had been working for Monk for three years. Getting his cabaret license back the year before had made things easier. As the saying goes, If you can make it in New York, you can make it anywhere. And if you can't play in New York, well then, things are a little compromised for the rest of the world. So this was one less headache. Then that spring, it was time to renegotiate his three-year contract with Riverside. Things were going smoothly, for his advances on royalties had more than doubled, and the percentage of record-sales money was increasing as well. Monk was now worth money, and he could feel he was going to be worth lots more. And this feeling helped wipe out the bad memory of the $108 check of three years before. This also meant that Thelonioous Jr. could go to an expensive private school and get a first-class education. Things were taking a good turn for the Monk family.

And then, in August 1958, the *Downbeat* magazine critics finally gave in and crowned him Musician of the Year. He was well on his way. He had a good producer, a good agent, money, recognition, beautiful music, and the feeling that he had made it by determination and not by luck or compromise. So many others have died before getting that far. Well, of course, there were those moments of absence—he could wander through the city without knowing where he was going, or who he was. There were those days and nights on end when he would pace back and forth in his room until he collapsed from exhaustion. And there were his long periods of silence when he didn't even speak to his wife or children. But we'll get to that later.

‖ 8 ‖

Saxophones!

Of all the instruments, the saxophone has come to symbolize jazz (oddly enough, for only the drums were specifically invented for jazz, but that's another story). The epic tale of this instrument was recently celebrated on the occasion of its 150th birthday so I won't go into detail, but a few words should be said about its importance when Monk burst upon the scene. In the mid-1940s, the four basic jazz wind instruments were the clarinet, the trombone, the trumpet, and the saxophone. The clarinet, the undisputed star of "classic" jazz, was becoming the emblem of outmoded music when bebop appeared, despite its exceptional color and expressiveness. The trombone, with its superb range, is difficult to handle in the highest and lowest registers, as well as in fast tempos. So for technical reasons, aside from a few outstanding soloists, the trombone never achieved the popular success of the trumpet or the sax, the two heroes of bebop.

The trumpet may not have a very broad range, but it dominates in the upper register, and that's enough to give it the lion's share. Its velocity, and bright or muffled quality depending on the use of a mute, made it an indispensable element of jazz in the hands of musicians like Dizzy Gillespie, Howard McGhee, or Fats Navarro. Then there's the saxophone. It's a simple-enough instrument to learn. Passing from bass to treble notes can be done with great facility. The fingerings are easy enough to allow fast, fluid phrasing; and above all, it is a reed instrument, and doesn't make the same physical demands on the lips, the air column, the diaphragm, and the abdominal muscles which the trumpet mouthpiece does. Also, it's an instrument on which each note corresponds to a position of the hands; while the trumpet, by using the proper lipping, can produce a half-dozen different notes with a single fingering

During World War II, jazz clubs had to pay an extra tax if they featured dance music or singers. By the end of the war, the big bands had gradually given way to the small ensembles which were the standard fighting units of the boppers. So the typical setup became: rhythm section (piano, bass, drums), plus soloists such as sax and trumpet. In tighter financial circumstances, as was frequently the case, a club owner or a tour organizer might only be able to pay four musicians, instead of five. Since you couldn't touch the rhythm section, the choice had to be made between the sax and the trumpet. But it's almost impossible for a trumpet player to be the only front man for three-or four-hour-long sets without damaging his lips. Even today, there are very few trumpetists who perform in quartet without the indispensable support of a saxophonist. On top of that, the sound of the saxophone is smoother and less taxing on the ear than the trumpet. For these and so many other reasons, it has become the king of modern jazz.

Monk, too, followed this rule and throughout his life he cultivated saxophonists, that primordial and vital species that would come to enrich his music. Or rather to enrich themselves from his music. Because being in his band was like going to school. And to question Monk's authority in his own band was like trying to blow up the White House with a cherry bomb. Right away, people went to Monk's band to play, and to learn. He even wore a ring with his name inscribed MONK—which, when you saw it upside down, read KNOW. No one ever dreamed of questioning his authority or his knowledge. Monk is a master, that's all there is to it. And that's why his encounters with saxophonists are so interesting, because he forces them to redefine their playing style, to reevaluate their approach, and to fit themselves into his tight but inspiring mold. Hearing Monk's music played by someone else is always a refreshing experierience, for it highlights his unique piano style. Monk invents a world which he alone can express effortlessly and naturally. In most cases, on some of his compositions, the other soloists have to run the equivalent of a 400-meter hurdles in order to play an original idea which doesn't sound corny.

One man alone was an exception to the soloist's natural allegiance to Monk—the master of them all; the one who, as Louis Armsrong did for the trumpet, raised the saxophone to full-fledged solo status and established its pedigree—Coleman Hawkins, aka "the Bean." From the moist marshland of the reeds came the cry of a great male voice. Bean was one of the Elders. Monk had barely begun to shave when Hawkins' definitive version of "Body and Soul" was recorded in 1939. It also happened to be one of the best-selling records in the history of jazz. Hawkins, master of the tenor sax, with his unforgettable sound, and his subtle, virile, and luminous phrasing.

He was also Monk's first studio employer. In 1944, a recording came out entitled *Bean and the Boys* which featured four tunes: "Flyin' Hawk," "Driftin' on a Reed," "On the Bean" and "Recollections." Monk played a sixteen-bar solo (the short format of the day) which left no doubt as to why the great Hawk hired him for his band. He had all the signs of an original and determined pianist, one who would become truly exceptional. And Hawkins was one of the rare musicians of the "classic" period of jazz (he had played alongside Louis Armstrong in the Fletcher Henderson band) to have maintained an active and kindly attitude toward the young boppers who were redefining the rules of the game. He recorded tracks with Dizzy Gillespie, Max Roach, Fats Navarro and Milt Jackson which proved his desire to modernize his phrasing, to expand his horizons and to learn from the new generation the things that the older one couldn't teach him.

Monk and the Bean both had a preference for arpeggio phrases, which had become rare in the "new" piano style of the day. Monk often backed his solos up with arpeggios—the separate notes of a chord—and not on the famous bebop scales and phrases which were being so widely used in improvisation. From the start, Monk seemed to base his style on a tradition common to his elders in order to develop it in a direction which he alone knew. And that "Monk color," which can already be perceived in the twenty-six-year-old pianist's strange melodic power, probably didn't disconcert the Bean any more than it did the boppers. Hawkins was on familiar ground with Thelonious—the land of the singing voice, the pointing finger, and the feet squared off. Scales had nothing to do with it—it was all a question of convictions shared with other musicians, regardless of age or style.

After this initiation into the recording world, Monk became a more or less regular member of Bean's band. He played with him on 52nd Street, and accompanied him throughout the 1945 tour of the States for the first Jazz at the Philharmonic concert series.

And Monk, I'm sure, had the undeniable satisfaction of knowing that he was recognized and appreciated by one of the legendary figures of jazz. Did this play a big part in his obstination to play his own music and not the music of everyone else? It's hard to say. But I can't believe that when you're young and you're playing in the band of one of the greatest musicians of the day, you don't take this as the confirmation of your own value, and the soundness of your own aesthetic choices.

Time goes by. Thirteen years later, in 1957, Thelonious is in his glory. He is now on the way to becoming one of the major voices of modern jazz. He can do as he pleases, for his fame is now well established. So what does he do? He gives old Bean a call, and returns the favor. For *Monk's Music* (Riverside, 1957), Thelonious is under no obligation to call in the old veteran whom others may have considered old-fashioned or inadequate. First of all, Hawk is nothing of the kind. And once again he proves his absolute mastery of all the colors, rests, and subtleties of the ballad form. Also, what a brilliant idea to put Hawkins and Coltrane side by side in the same studio—the old-timer and the newcomer, both in the service of Monk's ageless, eternal music.

The lucky owners of the complete Riverside recordings (four volumes, with all of Monk from 1955 to 1961) will find an excellent booklet in which Keepnews describes, session by session, the recording of everything Monk did for him. It's very precious, and instructive! When Keepnews mentioned the idea of *Monk's Music* to Thelonious, he proposed several saxophonists, but Monk turned them down immediately. Thelonious then suggested Coleman Hawkins, Gigi Gryce, and John Coltrane. The past, the present, and the future. No jazz producer could ever have come up with an idea so preposterous and fitting at the same time, unless he happened to be as brilliant as the artist he was recording. This was just another example of Monk's solid musical intuition. He always knew what was good, and what would sound right for his music. Keepnews also tells of how Thelonious was up for several days in a row preparing for the session, and was at the studio with unaccustomed punctuality. This showed how seriously he took the recording and how devoted he was to such an ambitious project.

I think this was also a sign of the affectionate respect Monk had for his former mentor. And he showed this affection right up to the end of his life. As Tootie recalled, a week never passed when he and his father didn't visit the old Hawk, who then had a long beard, and had been prematurely buried by jazz historians. The Bean was fried, they said, and was no longer sought-after in New York. And in his declining years, how greatly he must have appreciated the quality and elegance of Thelonious's loyalty.

Sonny Rollins was another saxophonist who diverged from the rule of allegiance to the master. Actually, though, he was a direct heir to Hawkins. And one important fact stands out— although Rollins, nicknamed Newk, was twelve years younger than Thelonious, he was one of the few musicians to have hired Monk as an accompanist. It took courage, admiration and an intimate understanding of Monk's music to decide to hire him for your own recording session.

Very few dared, as you can see for yourself:

Charlie Parker/ Dizzy Gillespie	*Bird and Diz* (Vogue, 1950)	Thelonious Monk (piano) Curly Russell (bass) Buddy Rich (drums)
Miles Davis	*Bag's Groove* (Prestige, 1954)	Thelonious Monk (piano) Milt Jackson (vibes) Percy Heath (bass) Kenny Clarke (drums)
Gigi Gryce	*Nica's Tempo* (Savoy, 1955)	Thelonious Monk (piano) Percy Heath (bass) Art Blakey (drums)
Art Blakey	*Art Blakey's Jazz Messengers with Thelonious Monk* (Atlantic, 1957)	Thelonious Monk (piano) Johnny Griffin (tenor) Bill Hardman (trumpet) Spanky DeBrest (bass)

Clark Terry	*In Orbit* (Riverside, 1958)	Thelonious Monk (piano)
		Sam Jones (bass)
		Philly Joe Jones (drums)

Plus Rollins, and that's it. At a time when everyone was playing with everyone else, when the whole world of jazz was in ferment, and when the discographies of his colleagues often covered several pages, Monk only recorded with six groups as an accompanist.

And why didn't they hire Monk as a sideman? He certainly played well enough. Lots of musicians thought he was a genius—all those stimulating chords, and that impeccable inner tempo. As Bud Powell's big brother, and the crony of Diz and Bird, he knew the jazz scene inside out. And by 1954, he had already acquired enormous technique and experience. The only thing was, it was great to listen to him, but having him in your band was something else. Because Monk played Monk, period. He could play anything, but only like Monk. Not like Al Haig, Bud, Tadd Dameron, or Teddy Wilson. And what he played was so strong that it would throw off any soloist who wasn't sitting tight in the saddle. If you played a brass instrument and had Monk behind you, it was like having the devil himself sticking his pitchfork in your ass—either it threw you off, or it gave you wings. Miles asked Monk not to accompany his solos on the only recording they made together (*Bag's Groove*, Prestige, 1954). That's perfectly understandable: you don't always want to have such a burdensome partner, especially when your name is Miles Davis, and your conception of rhythm, space and color is so different from that of Monk's.

But that didn't scare Rollins away. On the contrary, it inspired him. He is probably the only saxophone player who knew how to *use* Monk's support for his own improvisation. Others dreaded Monk's bursts of discordant inspiration. But Sonny took great pleasure in anticipating Monk's punctuations, and slipped in and out of them like a ship between reefs, coasting along as the spirit moved him. It was as if they could both hear the same thing at the same time. They were both New Yorkers, and had been breast-fed on the same music. As with Bud or Max Roach, there are some things you hear that just cannot be explained. The musicians of the bop generation came from everywhere. But when you were with other New Yorkers, you heard things in a certain way and that helped create a style. It's hard to define. Being a New Yorker gave you the aristocratic feeling of having been born into the right family, with a particular sense of honor and duty. For New Yorkers, the eclectic notion of concept is very important. Rollins, Monk, Roach, and Bud were all modern and classical at the same time. They were more like intellectuals than entertainers. This would account for the immediate empathy between Sonny and Thelonious.

The perfect example is Sonny's version of "Pannonica" (*Brilliant Corners*, 1956). Their two voices blend and complement one another amazingly. They are both sure of themselves and unpredictable, and share the same instinct for individual notes. Rollins finishes a spiraling phrase with the very note on which Thelonious chooses to build his accompanying chord. You can't prepare that kind of thing. It's like a rough, warm telepathy bouncing back and forth melodiously from one bar to the next. Rollins's way of picking out one note and accenting it repeatedly is so close to Monk's angular accents that you wonder who is accompanying whom. Then, Sonny reveals the full extent of their complicity by suddenly bringing the lyrical flight of his solo to an end and landing it right in Monk's hands. Fascinating. This commanding balance which united Monk with a saxophone player had never happened before, and would never happen again.

This is even more striking when Thelonious is the host—for the magnificent assurance of Rollins's phrasing could be fully appreciated over the course of Monk's compositions (and not the easiest ones at all). As I mentioned earlier, the nature of Monk's tunes forbids the soloist from indulging in ready-made phrases. Rollins and Monk share the same way of seeing things from *above*. Neither of them are anxious to struggle with a tune. They don't run out of breath, and only speak up when they have something to say. They both maintain the critical distance necessary to enjoy the occasional hitch, or to take a shortcut when needed. Or to hammer away at one corner of a chord with an absentminded light touch. Or to affectionately play a portion of the melody, then drop it on a whim. Monk and Rollins were made for each other. Instead of casting shadows on one another, these two giants dwelled together in a fond and fertile music.

Officially it was Thelonious who hosted first. He was then with Prestige, and called in Sonny for three tunes, in November 1953. The invitation was reciprocated in October 1954, again at Prestige, for two standards, "The Way You Look Tonight," and "I Want to Be Happy." Sonny's mastery, and his near-indifference to Monk's accompaniment, are stunning. (Who else could be? It was like swallowing a box of pins.) And Monk went right along with it in convincing fashion, playing his accompanist's role with fervor and modesty. Only on his solos could you hear the Big Bad Monk, true to his form. Magnificent work.

Brilliant Corners was recorded in 1956. Then in April 1957, Rollins called in Monk for a Blue Note record date. On this exceptional album, Monk shares the piano with Horace Silver, and backs up Sonny on compositions of his own ("Misterioso" and "Reflections"). The latter is particularly impressive in the way the two musicians converge in the same places, almost as if their telepathy were cumbersome. I wonder if it wasn't the presence of Art Blakey that made things even more complicated.

For this was the only time that these three jazz giants can be heard on a record together, and only on two cuts. Yet they have everything in common, which also set them apart from their contemporaries—the same immediate, almost brutal approach to music; the same miraculous sense of timing and precise phrasing; the same image of man as a rock, and jazz as a raging river, channeled by the musician's strength of soul. But that session of April 14, 1957, is the only little crumb of history that a collector can find if he wants to hear them together. Kind of strange. . . . Makes you wonder if putting them in a studio together wasn't dangerous—two of them, maybe; but three was asking for trouble. Just listen to the blues they play on "Misterioso," and you'll realize how intense this trio could be. And seeing them live must have been an unforgettable experience.

That session was the last to reveal the intimate complicity between Monk and Rollins. You can't help wishing that destiny had brought them together on records more often.

Then along came Coltrane, and *that* was something else. This would be something brief (six months) and extremely intense. In any case, with Coltrane, things were always intense. In 1957, he was ranked the number one contender to Sonny Rollins. The year before, *Tenor Madness* had been recorded, on which the two saxophone players faced off in a blues duel with all their energy, knowledge, and future at stake. In that main event, the two heavyweights battled furiously to a draw, and the only winner is the listener. They are both out of their minds. Rollins has been seeking his identity for years, and untiringly changes his sound, his approach, and his style. Coltrane seethes within as he seeks to harness the music that possesses him, and which he still can't quite control. And Monk showed excellent judgment in his choice of saxophonists. In succession, he picked out the two most voluble musicians around, and they had carried his music into far-distant and fascinating regions of the soul. Rollins had never seemed more relaxed, but Coltrane was more convoluted and feverish than ever.

Coltrane had come over from Miles Davis's band which had been highly successful for several years. He was leaving a sublime quintet, with Red Garland on piano, Paul Chambers on bass, and Philly Joe Jones on drums. Miles's lastest racing car was rhythm on wheels! And for two years, Miles had let him take the wheel regularly. He cruised smoothly through superb ballads and steady medium tempos; then ruled the road when he put his foot to the floor for the uptempo numbers. Water-tight. They didn't come any better. The only problem was Trane's heroin abuse. This annoyed Miles, who had cleaned up and could suddenly see success staring him in the face. He wasn't going to let a junkie wreck his life again. So he fired Coltrane, who went with Monk to replace Rollins, and Rollins wound up in Miles's band. A fair exchange.

And music was the only thing that Trane was interested in. As Miles so aptly put it, "He was just into playing, was all the way into the music, and if a woman was standing right in front of him naked, he wouldn't have even seen. That's how much concentration he had when he played." Coltrane was a spiritual person, who sought the exit leading upward; he was vertically oriented. And Monk's influence was like a trigger. Coltrane quit heroin cold turkey, and plunged into Monk's music with a rage. He stalked Monk's music from top to bottom. He went through it all, playing pieces which were written only for the piano and seemingly impossible for the saxophone, such as "Trinkle Tinkle." He ripped it wide open, then stuck it all back together and nailed it to the wall. Just to keep his mind busy so he wouldn't think about *that*. Or he would go back to an old standard like "Epistrophy" by Monk and Kenny Clarke, which had been heard around the clubs for almost fifteen years. By that time, the tune was usually played pretty laid-back. And Monk was the only one who played it as it was written — going up or down a half-tone every other beat. It was exhausting, so people had gotten into the habit of playing eight bars in D-flat, then eight bars in E-flat, and so on, without breaking their necks. Everybody, that is, except Trane, who played everything, all the time and at top speed. Trane would go down to the shop floor to see firsthand how the mechanics of a tune worked. He'd take the engine apart piece by piece, then put it all back together. To me, Coltrane worked like a miner, with a helmet, a pickax, and the tenacity of a warrior. Every day for six months. The voyage to the center of the earth—each day he dug a little deeper, and each day he would come back up to the surface with a load of priceless treasures.

He even pushed Monk out of the way: Take a stroll, man, I got it. You don't have to play the chords; I play them enough as it is. And then Coltrane would take off into his "sheets of sound" which had no specific rhythmic definiton, but were simply leaps from one chord to the next; one long breath which wound around itself as it rose, like a snake charmer's rope. Monk got in the habit of accompanying him very little, and used his silence to allow the tidal wave to rise and break, giving only an occasional oarstroke. He let Coltrane run his course, carried along by his own feats of strength. And by means of his complex and felicitous compositions, he helped deliver the tormenting music that Coltrane carried in the depths of his soul. As if the constraints which his music imposed were the very ones Coltrane needed in order to be free.

Fortunately, there are a few recorded traces of Trane's brief but fruitful collaboration with Monk. The three recording sessions at the time (April, June, and July 1957), are . . . Well, why look for words to describe them when you can listen to them? "Ruby, My Dear," "Trinkle Tinkle," "Well, You Needn't," "Nutty," "Monk's Mood," and "Epistrophy" (I'm only citing the ones on which Coltrane improvises with Monk). Run for cover! All are definitive versions. The lovely and moving complicity between Rollins and Monk is a thing of the past. Trane literally depossesses Monk of his music. This is armed robbery. Except for maybe the ballads, like "Ruby, My Dear" and "Monk's Mood." Coltrane plays like the worthy successor to Hawkins: the melody first. He respects and caresses the ballads and doesn't take off in a flight of arpeggios, unless the tune permits it. A perfect proof of love! The tender weakness of the killer who renounces the kill when he falls under the spell of his victim's beauty.

Also, bringing the two musicians together in a recording studio was not easy, from a legal standpoint. At the time, Coltrane was under contract with Prestige, which Monk had left three years earlier under unpleasant circumstances. And when Keepnews called Bob Weinstock to "borrow" one of his artists, Weinstock said, Sure, if you lend me Monk (who was starting to sell). Monk wanted Coltrane for his record, but going back to Prestige was out of the question. So they met a little like lovers, in secret. And their musical tryst bore illegitimate children in the record world. One was "Monk's Mood," a single cut from one session, that later strangely appeared on his solo album *Himself*. Another is *Monk's Music* with Hawkins and Gigi Gryce, but Coltrane's name doesn't figure on the original cover. It's all kept very discreet. And then a last one in quartet on a label called Jazzland which added little gems to the album from the session with Hawkins. On these, Coltrane is so dominant that I wonder if that's not the reason why Keepnews didn't bring them out on Riverside.

A tape recorded live at the Five Spot by Naima Coltrane, of rather poor quality, recently came out on Blue Note. But who cares about quality, when you get to hear how things actually happened. Oddly enough, Trane is a little less aggressive than in the studio, and seems to leave more space for the piano, indicating that they were more than just teacher and student, and that a complicity developed between them over the six months, which grew as Monk's respect for his soloist increased. And Trane, caught up in the hurricane of his devotion to music, returned to Miles's band at the end of the year to complete a tale of love and ambition which had been left dormant. And only after turning that page did he fly off, rising ever closer to the sun, to fulfill his destiny.

In so doing, he left the way open for Johnny Griffin— the old buddy from back in 1948, the fourth musketeer of the infernal trio of Bud, Elmo, and Monk. In 1957, he was with Art Blakey and the Jazz Messengers. And in May of that year Blakey invited his old pal Thelonious to record with him on Atlantic. A warm reunion for Monk and Griffin. And, as Griffin was burning brighter than ever at the time, it was no surprise that he stepped in when Trane left in late 1957. The strangest thing is that by a stroke of fate, I have the feeling that Griffin was the perfect composite of Newk and Trane. For he had the rough sound, and the instinctive traditional lyricism of Newk, combined with all the unquenched ardor and rage of Coltrane. The authority of the bear and the fury of the lion—that is Johnny Griffin, the Little Giant.

Here again, as with Rollins, the two musicians shared a friendship which time never affected. Griffin was in the big band that Monk took to Europe in 1967. Coltrane was serious and searching; but Griffin was completely jubilant. There was no stopping him, either, but that's because he was having too much fun to cut his solos short. He loved Monk, and it showed in everything he played. He loved to frolic around inside the tunes which seemed to defy his ability to improvise.

And especially, it was with Griffin that Monk started to record live albums. For up to that point, the only things we heard from Monk were what the producers at Blue Note, Prestige, or Riverside were willing to let us hear. Monk's studio albums were usually made up of first or second takes, and only the very gifted ear can recognize the cutting-and-splicing job. The impossible *Brilliant Corners*, with Rollins, was made up of several portions from different takes. No single take was satisfactory enough to be used on the album. A similar process could be used for live recordings, as they reach the mixing table before the record is pressed. However, the inferior sound quality and the presence of an audience make some editing very hard. So the sound engineer has to limit his use of the famous curved scissors for cutting tapes, before splicing them together. I am sorry to disappoint the neophytes by revealing that records are rarely made in a single take. Today, thanks to the techniques of digital editing, some classical works contain more than three hundred cuts in a single interpretation! Jazz doesn't reach those extremes, but even so, a little intro here, an interlude there and you've soon made a half-dozen scalpel cuts for a single session—the plastic surgery of the record world. The nose of the tune sticks out too far? Just trim it back. Missing some backside? Throw some more on. One ear's bigger than the other? Just trim it. Yet this editing technique, combined with the appearance of magnetic-tape recording, was then in its infancy, and in the case of Monk in the 1950s, was only used rarely.

To get back to Griffin, he was the one who began the series of live albums. Today, such a recording usually takes place in the following manner: you pick a club or a concert hall where the band will be playing the same repertoire for several days in a row; you take a sound truck there; you tape everything, then you take the best version of each tune to make the record. At the time, the techniques of live broadcasting had been mastered, after years of radio programs. But making records was a different story. Norman Granz had launched the idea with his Jazz at the Philharmonic series after the war, but the technique still needed to be perfected, and the equipment was expensive. So to make a forty-minute album, you set up microphones for one night and the band played the same tune several times in order to get a good take for each one. This was rudimentary, and frustrating for the audience, but efficient. The age of "live recording" had begun.

At the time, there was a big difference between the music you could hear on record, and the music you could see in a club. Not in quality, but in quantity, and that means a lot. Let's go back a bit. When Monk recorded for Blue Note in 1947, the only records available were the famous 78 rpm's. Their playing time could vary from three minutes for the 10-inch records to four and a half minutes for the 12-inch. Three minutes. The length of one round in a boxing match. They say that after three minutes, the professional boxer's acute-concentration span starts to wane. He's not the only one. The whole world is built around three-minute cycles. Even today, popular songs are usually three minutes long. It's not because the records are too short, as compact discs can last an hour and eighteen minutes, but because people's minds start to wander after three minutes. And a lot can happen in 180 seconds. Beyond that limit, you start to balk and daydream, and before you know it, you are no longer paying attention at all. So, up to the late 1940s, all the masterpieces of recorded jazz are three minutes long (or, occasionally, four and a half minutes).

In fact, this format was fine for the small bands. An introduction (between five and ten seconds long), the melody (as much as one minute, for slow tunes), two or three solos (a minute and a half, maximum), then the whole band taking the melody home (for whatever time remained). With this format, you didn't have time to get bored, and there was a little something for everyone: nice melodies, well played, compact solos, and a good blend of instruments. What more could you ask for? For Monk, it was more than he needed. As the master of concision, he felt perfectly at home in this structure. He had plenty of time to surprise the ear. Anything more would have been too much!

Then, in 1948, the long-playing record appeared. Columbia and Capitol registered trademarks respectively for 10-inch 33$\frac{1}{3}$ rpm and 7-inch 45 rpm. records. Recordings were now five times longer. Wonderful new horizons apeared: classical works could be recorded in a single shot, without having to change the disc every four and a half minutes. As for jazz, more varied formats, longer solos and more complex approaches were possible. One basic principle never changes: A new technology means a new jazz. Now, instead of offering small musical vignettes (a little sax, a little trumpet, right this way, ladies and gents, watch your step, please), the new formats made it possible to go into depth and provide a more serious and complete image of jazz. From the mid-1950s, you started hearing six-, or even ten-minute tunes. One example is the session that Miles Davis did on Prestige with Monk on piano, on Christmas Day 1954. The first tune, "Bag's Groove," runs for 11 minutes 6 seconds. Plenty of time for everybody. Mind if I take another solo? By all means; the pleasure is all mine! A few years before, they'd have been on the fourth tune by that time!

A few artists jumped at the chance and immediately

took advantage of the new possibilities, including Duke Ellington, Miles Davis, and Horace Silver. Monk couldn't care less about new techniques. As his music was already three thousand years old, a few minutes more weren't going to make any difference. So before 1957, aside from rare exceptions, he said everything he wanted to in about five minutes. Of the twenty extra minutes that the LP gave him, he usually used only one. There were two remarkable exceptions: "Just You, Just Me" (1956), and the amazing "Friday the 13th" with Sonny Rollins (Prestige, 1953), written on a corner of the piano, then immediately recorded one Friday the thirteenth. A special tune for a special day. Up to that time, this was the longest piece he had ever recorded—10 minutes 31 seconds. But it was also the shortest he had ever written. The melody was four bars long, repeated over and over. For improvising, there were four chords in two bars, also repeated ad infinitum. Here, Monk illustrated the paradox that the infinitely large can be contained in the infinitely small—which resolves the problem of length in an unexpected but dazzling way (and, that's just how I imagine a bad-luck day like Friday the thirteenth : a broken record that you just can't seem to change).

So Monk only rarely made use of the "large format." It was only in late '56, when he recorded *Brilliant Corners*, that he let himself go for a whole album, with extended tunes like "Pannonica" (8 minutes 50 seconds), "Brilliant Corners" (7 minutes 46 seconds), or "Ba-lue Bolivar Ba-lues Are Ba-lue" (13 minutes 24 seconds). He was ready to dive into the huge world of live recording. But if, up to that time the tunes were long, it was because they adhered to simple but strict rules: a melody, solos of identical length for each of the soloists (once or twice through the changes), maybe a few bars for the drums, and one last time for the melody. And when tunes lasted for more than five minutes, it was because the form was longer than usual—nothing you can do about that. You were still working within a format which aimed at concision. But all that changed with the LP. The difference in length between a radio broadcast, a club performance, and a record was done away with once and for all. Now you had concerts at home, and records in the clubs. With all this multimedia interactivity, things were starting to get complicated!

And this raises all kinds of questions. For what is the *real* difference between a live album and a studio recording? Is it the same music? Does the presence of an audience change the way a musician plays? Or is it the studio atmosphere which lets you do certain things you cannot do live? To find out, you'd have to examine the conditions of these two types of recording in detail. Let's follow Monk into the studio.

A producer organizes a studio session to record some tunes. A day and a time are set, and the musicians show up separately, more or less on time. Then Monk arrives. Now, either the band records tunes they've already played, or there are new compositions. With Monk, you never know. He says a few words about the tune, then plays it on the piano. The bass, drums, and saxophone join in. Then the producer starts the tape rolling, but suddenly has second thoughts, and calls down, "Is this a take or a rehearsal?" "Hold on, let's start again; I'm rewinding. . . ." Meanwhile the saxophone player checks his reed and blows a couple of riffs, and the bass player tunes up and goes over a tricky change at the bridge.

"Okay, the tape is running." They start the tune, then stop after eight bars, as Thelonious knows just what he wants for the introduction but it's obviously not clear to the other musicians. "Yeah, right," one of them says; "we play the the A twice, okay let's go."

Take two. They play it all the way through. As soon as the last note fades, a voice in the headphones says, "That one was good; you want to listen to it, or do it over right away?" They decide to play it again. Take three. Not bad. Not as good as the second, but the head is better. "Shall we do another take?" "No, that's enough. I think we've got what we want. Okay. What's the next tune? Ready. . . ."

In the studio, you get progressively into the music, and you can fool around with your instrument and work out some ideas before the tape starts rolling (there's a particularly eloquent version of "Round Midnight" on Riverside). All of a sudden you realize you're about to record, but you ease into it. A little like fixing your pillow before you lie down for bed. When playing "live," on the other hand, you have to give it everything you have right away. Forget about the little flaws, everybody's on the job and you have to make it *sound*. You also have to beware when you're playing for an enthusiastic audience, because you want to push it to the limit, and if you don't pay attention, you can do some damage. It's like pushing your way through a crowd, and stepping on a few feet as you go.

It is obvious that a musician's attitude to his music undergoes a change from the stage to the studio. In Monk's case, you can't really say it affects him much. The world may well revolve around him, but he doesn't move, no matter what happens. But it was live recordings that helped him find a comfortable, standard five-to eight-minute format, free of the tyranical restraints of the 78 rpm records. Gone are the four-minute gems all stuck together on collections; the precise, radical little arrangements, the half-solos, the left-right combinations that really knock you out. Space has taken over again—whole solos with no piano accompaniment; lengthy keyboard work: the same riff hammered out over and over.

So Keepnews decided to put microphones onstage at the Five Spot, and to inaugurate the system of live recordings with Monk. And Griffin is the perfect man for that. What a fight: the High Priest of Bebop versus the Little Giant. Ice against fire; the net versus the trident. The jazz gladiators. In fact, it was more like tag-team wrestling, as Roy Haynes and Ahmed Abdul-Malik didn't remain in their corners, either. In this "battle royale," the whole band fought it out to see who could swing the toughest, the strongest, and the longest. It was as if the band was striving to pick up the pieces and patch things up, in the wake of Hurricane Coltrane. That's the way it was throughout the summer of 1958.

A studio recording session had taken place with Griffin in February of the same year, which turned out to be a huge catastrophe. The only tune they recorded, "Coming on the Hudson," was among the most treacherous Monk had ever written. A five-bar melody, with a three-and-a-half-bar bridge, wasn't exactly standard format at the time. Despite Griffin's goodwill, everyone was lost. Thelonious himself kept skipping two beats in his solo, which only made matters worse. The gods of music, better known as gremlins when they disrupt a session, must have all ganged up against this project. Blakey and

Rollins never even showed up, and the piano Monk was playing on collapsed when one of its legs broke off after the first take of the first tune. That was enough for Thelonious. He knew how to read the oracles, so he went back home to bed.

‖ 9 ‖

Full-length Portrait

When Griffin left Monk's group in late 1958 to return to Chicago where his family lived, Thelonious was in the public eye. His reappearance on the club scene for the past year had allowed jazz fans to get to know this strange pianist whose imposing figure immediately struck the imagination. Hearing him was one thing, but seeing him in person was a true spectacle!

Even his name set him apart. Like all determined individuals, who give the impression of having a good reason for everything they do, Monk bore his name like he wore his hats—with full confidence. He often used it in his compositions: "Monk's Mood," "Monk's Point," "Monk's Dream," or more indirectly "Oska T" (a phonetic transcription of "Ask for T."). Like Caesar referring to himself in the third person, Thelonious seemed to point an affectionate and ironic finger at himself. And this has a lot to do with the mythology of the jazz world, where musicians give each other nicknames—

Satchmo, Bird, Diz, Trane, Bags, Bean, Prez, or Newk. Like a second birth certificate. How many people know that Duke's real name is Edward Kennedy Ellington? But with a custom-made name like Monk, no need to look any further. He came into the world with his stage name. He could only be called Monk, or Thelonious, or simply T.

Also, the word itself carries a mystical dimension, and conjures up a particular setting and lifestyle. The monk (and not the priest, the apostle, or the hermit) is a pictorial figure who evokes both respect and amusement. A monk is a funny blend of opposites: a solitary individual who belongs to a group; he is both somber and colorful, poor but well-fed, bald but bearded. Miles's name was used throughout his career either as a pun or because of its assonance, in titles like *Milestones, Miles Ahead*, or *Miles Smiles*. Monk never played with the ambiguity of his name and never used it as a reference to anything but himself. Yet, the name has a universal ring to it, like the name "Kodak" which the Eastman company chose because it was easy to pronounce in any language. But even Americans have a hard time with "Thelonious." This strange combination of a universal family name and a singular first name is rich enough to make puns unnecessary. When the producers suggested he wear a cowl for the cover photo of the album *Monk's Music*, he refused categorically. He had just bought a beautiful two-hundred-dollar suit and couldn't understand why he should have to play the clown in a sackcloth bag with a curtain string. Monk was Monk. No need to rack your brains for a nickname, and if Thelonious was good enough, well, then, God and his family, in their infinite generosity, had also given him the middle name Sphere. That should do it.

Physically Thelonious stood a good six feet two inches, and weighed around two hundred and twenty pounds. I say "around" because of his penchant for spinning around to express his satisfaction. With age, Monk got harmoniously rounder which made the name Sphere all the more appropriate. The passing years definitely gave him an overwhelming and circular authority. Some people grow lean with age, like Hank Jones or Art Taylor; or huge, like Mingus; or haunted, like Mal Waldron; or ageless, like Herbie Hancock. Monk came to resemble the perfect patriarch. Even if he had never as much as threatened to throw a punch in his life, people approached him with awe. For a long time, the story went around that Miles had asked Monk not to back him up on his trumpet solos during the famous Prestige recording session of Christmas 1954. Thelonious got angry at Miles, so the story goes, and bawled him out. First of all, that would be completely out of character for Monk, and, as Miles said in his memoirs, you'd have to be nuts to pick a quarrel with Monk! He virtually filled the room. He was full-chested, with a broad back and a frame that could support incredible weight and stress. He had solid legs, planted in his characteristic wide-spread stance, with his feet pointing out. Built to last.

Despite his heavy, bearlike appearance, he was deceptively quick and a formidable Ping-Pong player. He put all his weight into every shot, and gave the ball a trajectory as unorthodox as the moves he was making. Teddy bear suddenly turned into Spiderman. He also excelled at pool, which requires perfect use of one's weight. And his driving was definitely impressive, in all senses of the word. His unpredictable moves and deceptive inertia often put his passengers in a cold sweat. He ran red lights, skidded in the snow, and slammed on the brakes (he did have one accident which was serious enough to put him in the hospital in 1957). Onstage he appeared somewhat clumsy. But when he was happy with the music, he'd get up from the piano during the other solos and start dancing, to his fans' great delight. He'd take a few steps, then suddenly spread his arms and give the impression of weighing four hundred pounds. He'd start to keel over just for a second, catch himself, then raise his foot only a few inches but make it look like he was about to fly away. Only Monk could give such a sense of balance with so much weight. He seemed to defy the laws of gravity. He could make density dance. And when it was his turn to play, he'd race back to the piano like he'd left something on the stove and launch into the first notes of his solo. Then he'd play and play and his music kept on dancing, advancing, falling back, and doing somersaults like he'd never get to the coda in time, but he did, and when, carried along by his momentum, he seemed to reach the end before the others, just when it looked like he'd be there all by himself,—no, he was just kidding, he crossed the finish with all the others, suddenly easing up; and, with his head bent attentively to the keyboard, he seemed to be giving a roguish wink to the other musicians.

It is touching to see him move like that. He floats, he sails, and he cruises and tacks like a yacht. He never hits the microphones or gets his feet caught in the wires and never makes an awkward move. His sense of balance is unorthodox, but is infinitely more mischievous and playful than the norm.

And he was always well-dressed. His taste was impeccable and as soon as he started making money, he was always dressed to kill. With his fine quality suits, shoes, shirts, and overcoats, he had a natural elegance as if to the manner born. He often kept his jacket and overcoat on when others were in shirtsleeves, like someone who was simply on a visit, making timely comments which were often cryptic but always witty.

People are still talking about his carefully selected hats. In the course of his travels, he had accumulated a vast collection of all sorts—oval, round, pointed, felt, fur, shiny, or soft ones, Monk had hats for all occasions. His headgear was as much of a bebop trademark as Dizzy's beret and glasses. Back then, you either got "hip" or you were nowhere. And a well-chosen hat was the best way to start. You had to think modern. For Monk, being modern was essential, as he often said during his debut with Blue Note. And the things he put on his head must have influenced the way he thought.

A hat is like a circumflex accent on one's personality. And in Monk's case, it's worth paying attention to. The rest of his attire was always classical, a far cry from the attempts at originality of Miles or Roy Haynes. In itself, this is an obvious metaphor: his style was traditional up to the neck. After that it was 100 percent Thelonious, and the hat was there as a reminder. He always insisted on the fact that inside his head was where things really happened. He wasn't into luxury watches, crocodile-skin boots, or artistic neckwear. What interested him was the head and its gray matter composed of little modern cells. His hats were provocative. In 1954, when he first went to Paris, a cartoon in *Jazz Hot* magazine portrayed him as a sphinx. The enigma. Inscrutable. Beneath the void was the meaning. His hat seemed to say: Go ahead, listen, think about it; something interesting's going on here.

Wearing a hat requires a certain reserve and aloofness;

otherwise it can make you look ridiculous. Monk met the challenge. I would even say that his hats gave an habitual dignity to the playing of his music. In 1971, when he took part in the "all-star" tour produced by George Wein, with Blakey, Al McKibbon, Sonny Stitt, Dizzy, and Kai Winding, for the first time in a long while he was an accompanist and didn't wear a hat. As he was no longer the leader, he didn't need a hat. It's almost heartbreaking to see him in the photos of that tour with nothing on his head. It's as if he'd been stripped of his command. Usually before each concert, the audience stirred with anticipation wondering what he would wear. And when he came onstage, people were thrilled as much by the hat as by the man. And at the end of his life, when he no longer touched the piano, he stopped wearing hats altogether.

Unlike a military hat, which is designed to remove any trace of individualism from the person who wears it and to define the man by his function, a hat on Thelonious produces the opposite effect. I even wonder if, when he had become famous and everyone "had heard of him," people didn't recognize him because of his hat, rather than in spite of it. He changed hats all the time, but you knew right away it was him. Some musicians like to establish a permanent public image, like Gato Barbieri with his dark glasses and his inevitable broad-brimmed hat. But that logo is a marketing ploy so that the record will be more noticeable on the store racks. With Monk it was different: he was never pictured with the same hat twice. As usual, he was ever-changing. In fact, he wasn't wearing a hat, but the idea of a hat.

And each time it seemed to give him a different face. He looked imperious in a sealskin schapska; pensive in a hunter's hat, as on the cover of *Time* magazine;

inscrutable in a Vietnamese straw hat; relaxed in a simple cap; somewhat dazed in a white panama; or all smiles in a beret. His expression could be completely absent as if he had retreated deep within himself. Or its childlike bliss and innocence could be immediately contagious. Or he would mischievously stick out his chin, like he had just played a joke on you. A quick, stern glance from Monk could plunge his entourage into an embarrassed silence. Although Thelonious's face was not what one would call expressive, his half-smile was full of understatement and irony. When he spoke, he didn't raise his eyebrows, nod his head, or use any of the little indications to enhance meaning, which is why people can understand Italian without having learned it. Monk just let the words fall in a tongue-in-cheek manner.

He had a broad, flat nose, full lips, and a prominent chin. His face was fleshy and his skin was a deep black hue. His ears were tiny and well-formed. Neither handsome nor homely, he stood out in a crowd because of the extreme intensity of his presence: he radiated power, he commanded. Onstage he didn't even speak to his musicians—no need to, as everything was in the music. He often let the trio sax, bass, and drums play alone for extended periods. He danced when the music was good, or left the bandstand when he thought something was lacking. The intensity on the bandstand had to be kept up or Monk wouldn't return. Art Taylor told of a concert he played with Thelonious one night. Things were going so well that in the middle of a tune, carried away by the general enthusiasm and fear of missing out on a solo at an intense moment, he call out to Monk, "Hey, T, give me some!" But Monk kept right on playing and brought the tune to a close without giving in to the drummer's request. In the fervor of the moment, Art Taylor must have rushed the beat or slowed it down, putting the rest of the band in a vulnerable position. Monk's reply didn't require words. But to make his point forcefully—which he rarely did—he went up to the microphone, and when the applause died down, he said in a solemn voice, "And now, our drummer would like to take a solo."

Which meant that if you let yourself go too much, he didn't like it and he no longer felt like playing. And if things really went wrong, he'd go back to the piano and take things in hand. With a few notes, the tempo would imperceptibly slide back to where it was supposed to be. A few of his 500-volt chords, and the band was immediately charged up again. Both onstage and in daily life, he gave off an irresistible directorial strength which had no need of words. Monk believed in silence, both in his life and in his music.

Silence can often be synonymous with absence or emptiness. You have to speak up in order to exist. These days, not talking means not thinking. But not for Thelonious. When trying to get four-year-old children to sing together, the hardest thing for a teacher is to make the child understand that when he isn't singing, the song continues rhythmically, and that silence is not a suspension of the tune, but a reserve of inspiration, of ideas, and of music. Monk believed in that inexhaustible reserve of silence. He *heard* the music as much as he played it, and there aren't many musicians who do that. What's the use of speaking? It's a luxury! He had a record player in his head that played all the time. So he could watch, feel, and listen without having to open his mouth! Hank Jones told of a six-hour trip he took with Monk and Bud, who were sitting next to each other. They never said a word the whole time, and when they reached their destination, each headed off to his dressing room, and Bud said to Thelonious, "Nice talking to you." That was typical! Those two didn't need words in order to communicate.

Thelonious didn't believe in words, for they change too quickly, and vanish as soon as they are uttered. Words are frivolous and can go off in all directions, and will mean tomorrow the opposite of what they did yesterday. Which is why all of Thelonious's words are *witticisms* —words which aren't merely self-serving. They are spontaneously humorous words which go straight to the heart of the matter, because they refute conventional meaning. I see Monk as a kind of Heraclites, who knows that everything changes, everything is in flux and flow, and everything is a subject of wonder and doubt. Then, on the other hand, was his music, and his certitude, which he refused to discuss. The mountain against the river. Monk didn't talk a whole lot in his lifetime, gave very few interviews and didn't have many lengthy conversations. He coined words, but spent them like a miser. Toward the end of his life, he merely grumbled. His face became an African wooden mask. Then, only his eyes spoke.

And when he did speak, it was with disarming frankness. He wasn't concerned with conventions or conversational gambits but went straight to the point. And so often, especially at the beginning of his career, his frankness was disturbing. Many club owners didn't care for that—who did this guy think he was? Gradually they got used to it. And people realized that with Thelonious, you just had to be yourself.

For he was one of the most uncompromising artists imaginable. He was totally in the music. He was never at a loss, and was always ready to play. This was an exalting, intoxicating feeling—the state to which all artists aspire—one of total and immediate communion with one's instrument. No dross, no lack of intensity, and no distance from the object. Everything he touched turned to art. When learning music, the technical difficulties of the instrument, the harmonic and rhythmic complexities, and stage fright are all obstacles to the musician's immediate enjoyment. Love of playing implies a love of pleasure. So, you learn and practice. And, certain musicians eventually attain a state of calm certitude of beauty and truth. The perfect balance between the effort and the result. Music pours through them with absolute fluidity. Great musicians are often truly calm individuals, for they possess an almost mystical awareness of energy. And that is exalting. With their grandiose alchemy, they can transform an object into music, like lead into gold. Monk was a supremely calm individual, but his energy capacity was so high that it was almost frightening. Energy vibrated all around him, giving off a diffuse aura. Then it all suddenly fell into place and became focused the moment his fingers touched the keys.

Hands. A pianist's hands are objects of universal fetishism. Like the nose of a wine tester, or the legs of a boxer. And yet a pianist also plays with his wrists, his neck, his respiration, and his elbows. And, of course, his feet. Monk's feet inevitably drew the attention of all the cameramen who filmed him in action. They seemed to have a life of their own, and reacted to his music in flourishes. His feet expressed all the tension that was released above them, and then buried those sounds into the ground which carried them. And his feet beat out the joyous tempo of the rough, exquisite music he was playing. But his hands were what really won the prize. Thelonious didn't really have what you could call pianist's hands.

They were not the magnificent hands of a pianist like Keith Jarrett. Jarrett's hands are unique—supple and muscular, agile and powerful—like those of an athlete; sometimes hesitant on the keyboard, but in such an instinctive way that they never lose their assurance and direction. Nor were they like the hands of Bud, with their fabulous spatulate fingers which caressed the keys instead of striking them, with the meat of his fingers, without the least sign of effort or fatigue. Or Oscar Peterson, with his two implements which seem to span half the keyboard. Or hands like those of Bill Evans—perfectly attentive, no superfluous movement, as if he were extracting a thin but constant flow of precious vital fluid.

No—Monk's hands were more like palms divided into five parts. Each fingertip semed to be all nail. His extraordinary nails once had to be cut during a recording session in London in 1971 (*The London Collection*, Black Lion), because of the noise they were making on the keys. His hands were astoundingly small in relation to his size. His eminently personal technique was said to have originated because of this. He even had a hard time playing tenths on the piano. That interval, of about 9 inches, is the standard for measuring if a pianist is lucky or not.

Monk's hands weren't designed for making a fist, and an invisible force seemed to stiffen them straight out. And his fingers didn't have much of a spread. They liked to stay close together, for anything could happen—they could get stuck with a cigarette, a huge ring, or a glass of whiskey, picking up things like a rake. On the keys, they produced results which were unimaginable. One portion of the film *Straight, No Chaser* shows Monk, during a piano solo, pull a handkerchief from his pocket, take his cigarette from his mouth, wipe his sweat-soaked brow (with the cigarette still in the other hand), place the cigarette on the edge of the piano (where, of course, it burned the wood), then put the handkerchief down, improvising all the while, with handkerchief and cigarette in hand according to where he was in the changes to "Round Midnight"! He could do anything with those hands!

His hands were not strictly reserved for the piano, like the delicate hands of a diva. Before hitting the keys, they carried with them a space, a life, a void: *bang!* The field of action of Monk's hands was much more than the black and white surfaces of the eight octaves! In fact, it wasn't a surface, but a volume! One yard above, one yard to the side, one in front and one behind! Standing, sitting, leaning forward, not like Jarrett whose hands never leave the keyboard, but rather attacking the keys from a distance, from high above, as only he could do. The notes he played must have weighed over two hundred pounds! *Bang! Bang!* Or sometimes they weighed only a few grams, and were so faint that the transcribers refer to them as "ghost notes"—phantom notes that come to haunt the keyboard from time to time.

And he adored rings. Sometimes one on each hand, but always the famous MONK ring on his left hand. It takes practice to play with a chunk of metal like that on your finger! Especially since he often wore a heavy signet ring on the little finger of his right hand that would spin around when he was improvising, and that he would fidget with when he was ill at ease. You'd almost think he wore them on purpose to prevent himself from playing! When a piano player shows up wearing rings like that, you step aside—After you, please! His hands were paradoxical—they seemed crude, but they could delicately hold a butterfly by the wings. Those hands did nothing without a purpose. They weren't always sure of the results they would produce, but they were never feverish or frantic.

Sometimes he'd hit a chord on the keyboard, then immediately raise his arms as if he had received a jolt. Then he'd stare at the piano with a perplexed air as if to say, Hmm, that's weird; this thing sounds great. He always looked at his hands. Usually a piano player looks straight ahead and he can keep on playing when the lights go out. But *never* looked at his hands. He felt the keyboard and saw it in his mind, and touched it but never looked at it. In all the years that musicians have been surveying that yard and a half of notes on the piano keyboard, you'd think it would be perfectly familiar. But Monk would try some moves, cross his arms, then smash a note. He was always ready for something new to turn up. It was truly incredible the way he was able to maintain that contagious sense of naive amazement toward his instrument, right up to the end. As if the piano played all by itself. Or as if he made it speak in an unpredictable way, even for himself, by inventing rules as he went along. But even when hesitating, he always had a magnificent self-confidence. You'd never catch Monk playing those corny arpeggio runs into the upper register of the keyboard, the way so many pianists do, as if they'd suddenly turned into harpists. He always aimed at something specific, particularly the last note of an arpeggio. A couple of notes could disappear along the way, becoming ghosts, but never the last one!

With Monk, you are always heading somewhere. And when you get there, it's usually a big surprise.

‖ 10 ‖

Rouse, the Big Bands

Late 1958. At this time, Monk's music was starting to solidify. He had been scuffling for a long time, trying things out, changing record companies, and writing new tunes. There must have been days when he felt utterly spent. Now that his career had gained momentum, he began to unwind a bit. He dug into his old repertoire of original tunes and standards, strengthened his style, and set his sights on the future. He put on weight.

And at this point in his life, a musician appeared with whom he would be associated continuously. This would not be the occasional collaboration of someone like Art Blakey, but a permanent member of the Thelonious Monk Quartet. This was a true believer, a man for all gigs and seasons, at a time when Monk was playing more than he ever did in his life. His name was Charlie Rouse.

When Monk began a lengthy engagement at the Five Spot in early 1958, Johnny Griffin was the saxophonist of the group. And when he went off to do a few better-paying gigs with his own group, he just did what jazz musicians have always done and will always do—he sent a replacement, a sub for the night. One night he sent someone who evidently wasn't up to the task. The next day, Monk took him aside and told him, "Listen, if you're going to send a sub, make sure it's either Trane, or Rollins, or Rouse. But no one else."

Griff was surprised because he didn't think of Rouse as being in the same category as the other two. But Monk knew what he was doing. And when Griffin went back to Chicago in the summer of 1958 for a few weeks, he got Rollins to fill in for him. Then Rollins passed on the word to Rouse that Monk was looking for him, and left the group shortly afterward to pursue the trials and tribulations of his mystical quest. Rouse recalled that he was terrified at the idea of playing with Monk, but the offer was too good to refuse. So he braced himself and joined the band. And there he remained for almost twelve years.

Now, this is a sensitive point in Monk's career. Because everybody—from musicians to fans to philistines—all naturally had the same idea as Griffin. When the passing parade of the years had included Sonny Rollins, Milt Jackson, Clark Terry, John Coltrane, and Griffin himself, well . . . what can you say? . . . people had the impression that Rouse was a cut below the others. And yet, he was a remarkable saxophonist. The mere fact that he was ready to play a repertoire as challenging as Monk's was, meant he had to be top-notch. With the mad pianist throwing nails under your tires, you had to drive a tank and have nerves of steel. And Rouse played it all like it was a piece of cake. Don't forget that in the studio, Monk rehearsed his tunes briefly, then recorded in only one or two takes. For there to be a third take, something truly exceptional had to happen, like someone coughing during a solo. (Even so . . .) Almost everything that Rouse recorded in the studio with Monk was done in one take. But Thelonious had simply accustomed people to seeing him appear with the brightest stars in the galaxy—with musicians who had exceptional careers both before and after playing in Monk's band, people who were true giants.

But Monk hadn't exactly pulled Rouse out of the gutter. He was originally from Washington and had begun his career back in 1944 with Billy Eckstein, then had played with the big bands of Dizzy Gillespie and Duke Ellington, among others, as well as with the Count Basie Octet and the Benny Green Quintet. Not a bad resumé. It showed a marked preference for ensembles, rather than individual performance, a sense of teamwork and an ability to read and play charts—definitely five-star experience. Being a saxophone player in a big band is not an easy thing. You have to know how to blend with the other instruments to attain—as the *good* big bands do—a collective sound. And when the twelve or sixteen bars of solo come around, you have to say your piece quickly, then get back in line with elegance and cohesion.

The first time that Rouse can be heard on a recording with Monk is on the *Live in Town Hall* album (Riverside, 1959), ironically with a big band. He had been in Monk's quartet for over three months, but this was the first time they recorded together. And here, Rouse is breathing fire! He is in excellent company, too—but neither the casual ruggedness of Pepper Adams, nor the enormous, well-controlled drive of Phil Woods, nor the modern intelligence of Donald Byrd, prevent him from affirming his own personal style. His style is ethereal, in the way he lets his angular arpeggios flow and fall, without pushing them to the limit like Trane did. He plays everything with nonchalance. He can tirelessly ferret out little corners in Monk's tunes and tickle them with the tip of his reed. He builds up tension, releases it, then with a snap of the wrists he tightens the reins, and blows the swing phrase, with the genuine Washington, D.C., big, bluesy sound. He lays back for a moment, then leaps into swing again. In again, out again, Charlie took Monk's challenge very seriously. And he opens new inroads, with incongruous twists and turns, and sudden, clever dead ends.

Monk was enchanted. Just listen to him on *Five by Monk by Five*, (Riverside, 1959), the album which followed the big-band recording at Town Hall. On "Played Twice," you can even *hear* Monk listening to what Rouse is playing. That tune is one serious bed of nails for a soloist. The harmony and the melody become completely volatile. Farewell to the stable basis of tunes like "Straight, No Chaser," or "Rhythm-a-ning." This tune takes off for outer space. For a soloist, what seemed like a good idea only one second ago suddenly becomes a wrong note; the tonics rub up against the major sevenths shamelessly in broad daylight. This is a real minefield, and Thad Jones is the first to cross it. With all due respect, he doesn't make it through unscathed. I'm sure that didn't happen to him very often, for he certainly is an outstanding trumpet player and composer. But here, he hits a snag. Listening to it, I get the impression that Monk is doing more supervising than accompanying. But when Rouse comes in for his solo, you can feel Thelonious opening his ears wide. Rouse doesn't do a "stop chorus" like Griffin, or make tidal waves like Coltrane, or roar like Rollins. He zigzags in and out of the tune, always in the right place, never a wrong step, and you can hear Thelonious as an attentive butler opening and closing the doors. In, out. Taking his time. There seems to be a calm complicity which could go on for years.

But Rouse didn't have the Big Bad Sound, the kind that comes around only a few times in a century. He was simply an excellent saxophonist. And Monk's fans can be divided into two schools: those who like, and those who dislike, Charlie Rouse. For me, the question doesn't even come up. Rouse or no Rouse, if Thelonious chose him, then that's the way it was meant to be. He wasn't forced to hire him, and he knew what he was doing. I love his warm, intimate presence. But the real question is, Why did he stay for twelve years? No one else ever stayed with Monk for so long—why him and why so long?

Part of the answer lies in the reality of the times. Owing to circumstances, Monk hardly appeared in public for seven years of his life. Considering the quality of his music, he should have played much more. He'd have a concert here, a recording date there, but nothing which could keep a regular band together. In jazz, it's every man for himself, so the musicians who only play with a single group are exceptional. It takes a band that plays regularly and pays well to make a decent living. And when you're a sideman, you take what's around, you fill in the gaps, and you blend in. So when Monk would call the friends he wanted to work with for his concert tours or recording sessions, there was a good chance that one would be on tour in Europe, another in the studio with his own group, and the third wasn't answering his phone. When you don't have work, it's very hard to keep a band together.

But in 1959, the offers started to roll in. First, Monk

played at the prestigious Town Hall, then made his first appearances on the West Coast under his own name, then toured Europe in 1961 and Japan in 1963. Concert dates were coming in with a comfortable regularity. Now he could keep a steady band together. Especially if the money was good. And if one of his sidemen got another offer, he had to give Thelonious preference, otherwise he wouldn't really be considered as part of the group. So Rouse just happened to arrive at the right time—there was enough work for a whole year.

That would explain why he stayed for four or five years, but not for twelve. So the question remains unanswered. I've looked at it from every possible angle and can only conclude with a statement of the obvious: If he stayed so long, it's because he didn't leave. It sounds dumb, but when you think about it, you realize that the soloists who preceded him in Monk's band all quit to go off and follow their own careers. They were big, strong, restless creatures who came to drink for a while at the marvelous fountain of inspiration that Monk's music and Monk's presence meant for them. Then they went on their way toward further adventures. But Rouse came to Monk's band and found his place there. He unpacked his bags, and settled in for the duration. And that's why, due to circumstances, the passing of time, and the intrinsic demand of his style, Rouse was *the* saxophonist for Monk. The others were saxophonists *with* Monk, but not him. He got inside the music. He gave in to it completely, without hesitation. Sometimes Griffin gave the impression of struggling furiously, solo after solo, in a straitjacket. Rouse seemed like he was walking around in a robe and slippers, late on a quiet Sunday morning. He was relaxed and right at home. He didn't quibble over details as he had in the beginning of his collaboration with Monk—he took things as they came without getting annoyed.

I've even got a theory about that. In a jazz quartet or quintet of bebop derivation, the saxophonist and the trumpet player are front players. And if a pianist, aside from his work in a trio, is the soloist, it is so he can be equal to the horns, but not above them. He steps out of his role as accompanist to move up with the horns. Note for note, tooth for tooth. But still the piano is considered as part of the rhythm section. Just as a stool needs three legs, here is the most comfortable one in the history of music: piano, bass, and drums. You can take that anywhere. Under any conditions. Put whatever you want up front—oboe, English horn, cello, glockenspiel, sax, or flugelhorn—as long as the musicians are a little understanding, that rhythm section runs all by itself. As Rouse gradually found his place in the group and lost some of the fervor of his early days, Monk turned things right around. In his group, the piano had naturally become a purely solo instrument, while the saxophone became a full-fledged member of the rhythm section. It's as simple as that. People may say that's ridiculous, that when Rouse improvised, he wasn't accompanying. But I say he was. His style stays so close to the music, his phrases slide so smoothly and naturally through the harmonic labyrinth which Monk occasionally submits him to (for he had quickly dropped any idea of *exploration*), that it's Monk's accompaniment that can be heard and not Rouse's solo. Unbelievable! Even when he accompanied, Monk was the soloist. Like the drummer and bass player who spread an infallible energy throughout Monk's music, Rouse contributes to the war effort like the others and keeps up a steady pulse which both heats and illuminates Monk's playing. And by the same token, the band settled into an extremely stable power struggle. Monk no longer had anyone on his back. He reigned as absolute master. And the timing was perfect, because just then, in February 1959, he was going to treat himself to a piano player's dream: having his music played by a big band.

The Colomby brothers were the ones who set it up. And now that Monk was starting to be recognized, it was time to strike high and hard, time to play at Town Hall, New York City! The white man's Apollo! Call me Master! That alone could warm one's heart. It could be argued that this was not the first time that Monk had appeared at Town Hall (he had been there eleven years earlier, back in February of 1948), but this was different, for now it was under his own name and with a big-band formation. And when each note which is normally played on the piano is assigned to an instrument that amplifies and objectifies it, that is the ultimate. It's like having an army of musicians at your fingertips. General Monk! One for all, all for Monk! The Jazz Special Forces!

But had Monk been sitting down writing out all those arrangements for the big band (which was in fact six horns added to the regular quartet)? Pencils, paper, sleepless nights? I don't think so! No, because in life, Monk did *one thing*—he played piano. So behind this work there was a kingpin, a brilliant and devoted mind, an inspired servant of Monk's music by the name of Hall Overton.

And what a name ! Hall, as in Carnegie, and if you add an *e* you get "overtone." With a name like that, he was predestined. A former student of the Julliard School, and a pupil of Darius Milhaud, he put his knowledge and talent into Monk's service, and they began working together. Like a master tailor, Overton examined Monk's music in all its seams. And how do you play this chord? (Raise your arms please.) Do you want to hear the major third in this voicing? (A pocket on the side?) What's the tempo? (Have you decided on the fabric?) Who's going to take a solo? (Turn around, let's see how it fits.) For the accompaniment chords—legato or staccato? (Single or double stitch?) Et cetera. Thelonious took his music to be custom-tailored. Deluxe fashioning. A big band altered to the perfect fit for the immmense and majestic figure of Monk's music. What a challenge! It had to be strong and versatile—light enough for summer wear, and comfortable for the winter! Sturdy, adaptable, and elegant!

To do it right, Monk must have stripped his music naked; sat down at the piano and gone over the compositions in detail with his friend; taken the time to explain, and to make changes and corrections. Now, Dizzy was a born teacher, but Monk was more the type to play a tune through from start to finish until a person understood it. He never gave theories, examples, or exercises. He didn't take things apart and analyze them. No, Monk was a master, and however cryptic his word might be, that was what you had to go by. He let others do the explaining. Few musicians in Monk's small bands ever saw his original charts. But they all remember the listening effort and superhuman reflexes needed to understand Monk's music only by ear! Johnny Griffin told how it took him a week before he realized that "Light Blue," contrary to what he thought he heard while playing it, actually had a different set of changes the second time the melody was played. To my knowledge, the only musician to have said that Thelonious *talked* about his music was Coltrane. But I suspect that Coltrane, with his extreme attention to detail, probably asked more questions than he got answers to.

Be that as it may, the sheet music was usually right there in Monk's trusty bag. And a musician who was struggling with a difficult tune would eventually say, Come on, man, show me the music, it'll go faster. But the implacable Monk would simply play the tune again; or at best, he might grumble, I want you to *hear* my music, not *read* it. He was right. It had taken him weeks to write it; why should someone else deflower it in a few minutes? You have to be worthy of one of Monk's tunes—savor it, and learn for yourself how one note is longer than another, and corresponds exactly to that precise place in the tune. This wasn't like buying a prefab house, when you choose a ready-made set of blueprints. Here, you discover one room after the other, by the light of a candle, because the fuses blew out—Watch your step, I think the bridge is coming up on the right. This is the stone castle of the ancestors. It doesn't have all the latest comforts, but it sure felt good to be there. No telephone, no electricity, a little damp—but what charm it has, what spirit, what setting, and what a magnificent view!

So there they were—Monk and Overton, leaning over graph paper, measuring and designing the rooms. This might be a good time to shed a little light on one of the many mysteries in the mythological biography of Monk. According to some reports, he studied at the Julliard School, the summit of Western classical teaching. First of all, I never found a single trace of this episode (which doesn't prove anything), but it is certain that "classical" recognition is a well-known technique of jazz critics and historians who take their time in admitting the talent of an artist. He is retrospectively given a pedigree—academic palms, of a sort. But I can't really see how Monk would have had the time or the money to attend Julliard in his youth. And the tuition there was very expensive. Furthermore, I don't see why it's imperative to play classical music in order to be validated in jazz. And isn't that all beside the point? Thelonious read music and often enjoyed playing one of the numerous classical or jazz pieces of sheet music that were piled up on his piano. But why force him to enroll in an apprenticeship which can only decrease the immediate genius of his music? Monk doesn't need that. He played what he heard, and if that was something universal, well that's just too bad for those who, at all cost, try to place their ideas in little categories. That's the way art is! It doesn't always come out of schools, and jazz does so less than any other art.

In short, that Julliard legend may well have taken root in the fact that during those big-band rehearsals, Monk often stopped by Julliard where Hall Overton was teaching, and where it was convenient for them to work together. But this was when he was forty years old, and not twenty! He went there to teach, not to learn! He was the teacher's teacher. . . .

And what a sound. Monk by himself is exceptional, but this is Monk to the tenth power. There is no reason for his music to become sweeter or flatter when played by a big band—on the contrary. The angles are more acute, the curves are smoother, and the tempos have more presence. This is Monk language in the superlative voice! Oyez, oyez! Oh yeah! The idea of multiplying Monk by ten is that of a true jazz warrior, a megalomaniac. As if there weren't enough problems already!

So aside from Rouse and Monk, the soloists include Donald Byrd, Phil Woods, and Pepper Adams. Sam

Jones on bass and Art Taylor on drums round out the rhythm section. As for Eddie Bert on trombone, Robert Northern on flugelhorn and Jay McAllister on tuba, they don't take solos, but give a deep, brassy hue to the orchestration which is so essential to Monk's music. Overton's arrangements are perfect. The choice of tunes is daring and excellent, and Rouse's way of sliding between the chords of "Monk's Mood" is masterful. "Friday the 13th" is celebratory, and Phil Woods plays it with the perfect touch of exuberant charm.

"Little Rootie Tootie" should be rebaptized "Little Rootie *tutti*," as the band plays an ensemble section, at times harmonized, which is the exact solo that Monk had recorded six and a half years earlier for Prestige. This is a true feat—Monk's solo transcribed, practiced, and played by a big band. "Off Minor," a particularly difficult tune, was taken apart piece by piece by the methodically melodic Donald Byrd. "Thelonious" (his named employed in the big-band declension!) sounds like a collective profession of faith: Hail to the Chief! One man, one note! Thelonious for President!

The symphonic "Crepuscule with Nellie" is beautifully moving—Monk carries the whole band by himself, in a poignantly nonchalant rubato. This serenade to his wife, composed in 1957 when Nellie was in the hospital and Monk was left alone, can now be experienced in Technicolor and Panavision. And then, for an encore, another version of "Rootie Tutti," as the sound engineer hadn't started the tape running soon enough the first time, and missed the opening bars. Five seconds of music missing? No problem, we'll just do the whole thing over! And it's all good, new and extravagant. An unquestionable artistic sucess. The musicians certainly must have celebrated backstage afterward.

But the critics who covered the Town Hall concert didn't find the experience quite to their taste. They said it was poorly rehearsed. Mr. Monk is, of course, a very good composer, but is his music really meant for a big band? He should have written music appropriate to that formation, instead of recopying his chords verbatim, they advised, in their infinite wisdom. They added that the soloists weren't very inspired. In short, it was a well-done assignment, with a few mistakes, careful about the spelling, you can do better—I'll give you a B+ just because I'm generous. So, the other dates for the big-band tour were canceled, and five years would pass before this grandiose project was revived. This was a tough break, but Monk was used to such things. Then again, the concept of a big band which amplifies the pianist's playing was completely original. It had already taken time for people to get used to his piano style; and it would take a few more years to get the brassier version accepted.

In fact, the piano itself represents the whole orchestra. Any composition teacher can show it to you on the keyboard. Here is where the trombones are; the trumpets can go up to here, and the bass down to here.

That way, when you write music at the piano, you can always imagine that you have a big band at your fingertips. But here, it's just the opposite: It's the band that plays the piano! Overton's genius was his ability to harness the whole ensemble into the yoke of the piano.

But Monk had to close the big-band chapter, and to return to it later when people became accustomed to it and were, at last, ready to listen. He continued to record rich, exhuberant albums for Riverside. He tried out different rhythm sections. He played for a while with the masterful Roy Haynes, then with the impeccable Art Taylor whom he liked to victimize with his usual sense of humor. More and more work started coming in. Monk had reached a period in his life when he could begin to float. He played concerts in a variety of contexts, and was even asked to play for the annual dinner of the United Nations. He was looking around for his next group, and could be seen playing with the younger musicians such as Scott LaFaro, Elvin Jones, or Ron Carter. He brought saxophonist Steve Lacy into the band along with Rouse for four months in the summer of 1960. In Holland, he was given the Edison Award which he shared that year with Frank Sinatra. Obviously the barriers were coming down. Still trying to solidify his group, in that same summer of 1960, he finally found the perfect pair in John Ore and Frankie Dunlop. . . . Who? How come the great Thelonious Monk, in his well-deserved hour of glory, didn't put together a group of celebrities worthy of his renown?

I can see several reasons for this. First of all, if the name Monk was starting to be well-known on its own, then why associate it with others? From the start, Monk's one and only policy had been to find musicians who could play his music. Whether they were known or not, didn't matter. An "all-star" system meant nothing to him. And John Ore had excellent credentials, having accompanied, among others, Lester Young, Coleman Hawkins, Ben Webster, and Bud Powell. The same was true for Frankie Dunlop, who had played with Sonny Stitt, Rollins, Mingus, and Ellington. But neither one of them had been in the limelight. However, they produced exactly what Monk expected of them: an impeccable swing. Like a thick, luxurious carpet. It wasn't a racing car like Miles Davis's rhythm section, but rather a Cadillac—you just turn on the ignition and cruise.

And with this Pullman deluxe quartet, Monk left for Europe. He had been thinking about it for a while, and must have had mixed feelings about his 1954 trip to Paris. His manager had been talking about a European tour for several years. In '59 there was even talk of recording the music for the movie *Les liaisons dangereuses* "live" in Paris, as Miles had done for *Ascenseur pour l'échafaud*. As previously mentioned, it never took place, as the recording was made in New York, without an original score, and was finally rejected altogether. For ten years, Thelonious had seen all his friends make the trip to Europe, and heard them enthusiastically describe how they had been welcomed as artists, and not as blacks. (They were welcomed as both, in fact, but not with the same prejudices.) Kenny Clarke had settled in Paris, as well as Bud Powell. For Monk, there was no question of ever leaving 63rd Street, but he was anxious to go and see what was happening over there.

Thelonious had succeeded in doing something that would have been unthinkable a few years earlier. He had a regular band that was working steadily, and was going to play in Europe. Like the others. What seemed obvious for many of his colleagues had finally become ordinary reality for Monk—he had joined the jazz establishment. History had caught up with him. At the age of forty-three, Monk had become a respectable gentleman who fit into the usual circuits. Looking back, it seems normal, but at the time it must have been strange for him. So, in April 1961 he took his quartet for a two month tour of the Old World. Amsterdam, Paris, Marseille, Milan, Zurich, Berne, Stockholm, Copenhagen, and elsewhere! Then a whole tour of England, with Art Blakey and his Jazz Messengers on the same bill. Now he was definitely traveling in style. Everyone was delighted, from the musicians to the audiences, to the press (except in England, where his work was less well known). . . . By 1961, his records were being imported and distributed correctly, and were laying the groundwork for him. His time bombs were starting to go off all over the place, and his jazz melodies were reaching the ears of all international jazz fans. He was welcomed, and people listened to him with respect. On *Blue Monk,* the first few bars were drowned out by the enthusiastic shouts of the audience.

The band itself was perfection. John Ore is an unshakable rock. It would be hard to find a drummer who swings more than Frankie Dunlop; and Rouse is inspired and lyrical. Monk selected a repertoire of his old hits ("Round Midnight," "Epistrophy," "Rhythm-a-ning"), a few tricky ones ("Jackie-ing," "Off Minor"), solo versions of "Just a Gigolo" and "Body and Soul" just to lighten things up a bit, and, for his wife who was there backstage watching over him night and day, the sublime "Crepuscule with Nellie." The repertoire wasn't too difficult to play, it was running smoothly, and the Thelonious Monk Quartet had simply become a major reference on the international jazz circuit. At the 1962 Newport Jazz Festival, Duke Ellington did him the honor of inviting him up to play on his own compositions, and they played "Frère Monk," which Duke had composed for the occasion. In Baltimore, an angry crowd chanted, "WE WANT MONK—WE WANT MONK!" at a barrier the police had set up in front of a club which, by law, had to close at midnight. Monk's legendary delays were now an integral part of his concerts, and added an element of suspense which increased the listening pleasure.

As for his style, he had reached his classic maturity. More than ever, he created colors from his black and white keys; more than ever, he made his instrument sound as if he possessed it. Some people are born to suffer from the piano; but he was born to make the piano suffer.

The Riverside contract was reaching expiration in 1961, and it was time for Thelonious to see if his rating had increased. Indeed, indeed. Monk was now an international star. He was selling. He was dollars. But it didn't change his lifestyle in the least: he didn't buy a an estate like Miles; or move to Central Park West, like Blakey or Max Roach. He stayed right there on 63rd Street. But for the people in the business, as they say, he was starting to represent the opportunity for substantial profit. And there was a producer at Columbia by the name of Teo Macero who was making some very good records with Mingus, and with Miles. Furthermore, this label was the logical place for someone whose career was on the rise. It was a major, with massive means of distribution, and was ideal for Thelonious's art. Everyone now recognized Monk's genius. It became clear that, for both sides, the contract between Monk and Columbia was a marriage of convenience.

‖ 11 ‖

Columbia

Who made the financial decisions in the Monk clan? I'd say it was a toss-up between Harry Colomby, Nellie, and Thelonious; when it came to business, they all pretty much agreed. All three were practical-minded, not least Thelonious. Madman Monk, angel of eccentricity, nevertheless had a keen nose for reality. Making music was his number-one priority and, as he proved often enough, the idea of sacrificing it to mere money would never have entered his head. Even so, he knew his math, and when he played a club, he could estimate the take by counting the number of customers, minus overhead, and figure out how much was being skimmed off into the owner's pocket before his cut, seriously depleted, finally went into his own. Yes, Monk knew when he was being swindled. For years he'd watched it happen, even though he was playing the same music. In those days he had no choice. In 1962 it was a different story; now he could call the shots, lay down terms and make sure he got what was coming to him. Later on, he would transfer his publishing rights from Thelonious Music to Bar-Thel Music, in his children's names, and register his compositions with them. Not only was this a sound financial move, but it allowed him during his lifetime to leave a legacy to his survivors which even today guarantees Thelonious Jr. a very comfortable income—proving Monk not only had a shrewd head for business, but a strong sense of family.

So Columbia it was. The big leagues. It showed right away, not least by the amount of studio time they allotted him. Four days to record the first album, *Monk's Dream*. Five for *Criss Cross*, the second. Until that time, his recording sessions had lasted one or two days—Do it fast, get it right. Occasionally three, when they hit a serious snag, as with "Brilliant Corners" or "Played Twice." But four—total free rein—that was unheard-of! Then there was the sound: deep reverb, wide stereo; it was rich, luxurious, classical. In any case, Macero quickly adjusted it; this new sound was all wrong for Thelonious's music, and tended to freeze it. When I listen to *Five by Monk by Five* (his last studio recording for Riverside), followed by *Monk's Dream* (his first for Columbia) back-to-back, I can't help feeling a sort of rupture. Nothing radical; at age forty-five Thelonious wasn't going to change anything. But he seems to have taken a slightly new tilt, like a sailboat running before the wind and starting to list into the waves.

Up to then, his music had a youthful exuberance, its movement was jagged and unpredictable; on *Monk's Dream* he seems cooler, more levelheaded, and preoccupied by one thing: to swing hard and long. Gone are the wild leaps, arabesques, and other light touches. Time has expanded, its weave is looser. The group's ideas are prolonged continuously—the band jumps from the 400-yard hurdles to the long-distance race. The one original piece Monk brought like a bride's dowry for his first album with Columbia is a good example of this new direction. "Bright Mississippi" is a simple, very melodic tune. It has a sense of space, of prolonging the sheer joy of playing which never seems to end. "A disappointing work," some critics say. Not at all. I think it merely reflects the passion of the moment: Let's take all the time we need and swing till we drop.

And Teo Macero's contribution? Columbia made an inspired choice when it hired this saxophonist/composer-now-turned-producer. He and Monk knew each other; they'd even done a TV gig together in 1955, on the *Steve Allen Show*. For musicians like Miles and Mingus, Macero proved to be an acute and creative intermediary, tuned in to their needs and helping them bring off their most daring artistic ventures. In a big record company, it's nice to have someone in your corner who won't frown when you suggest calling in a sitar player for the next session. Monk was a different breed of cat; it never seems to have entered his mind to ask Macero's advice about what music he should record. Take it or leave it. He wasn't going to fiddle around with electro-acoustic machines or try out any strange new formations. He'd play what he'd always played and if Columbia liked it, so much the better. So Teo's influence was limited to discussing studio dates, or recording concerts "live" when the occasion arose.

At that time, Columbia's jazz production policy was simple enough, like that of Prestige ten years earlier: they recorded. Not much planning went into albums, the sales department took care of that. *Monk's Dream* and *Criss Cross* resulted from nine recording sessions held between October 1962 and March 1963. On the *Criss Cross* album, the six seconds between "Hackensack" and "Tea for Two," in fact, correspond to a time span of two and a half months! Even more surprising, Columbia's recording policy, for very different reasons (research, experiment) meshed perfectly with Monk's newfound focus (continuity, elaboration). Which just goes to prove the notion that Destiny never misses a rendezvous with itself. These first two albums include an assortment of pieces that they'd played many times over on concert tours, such as "Hackensack," "Rhythm-a-ning," and "Ba-lue Bolivar Ba-lues Are Ba-lue," a few numbers culled from the Riverside years ("Sweet and Lovely," "Blues Five Spot"), the Prestige years ("Think of One," "Monk's Dream"), even the Blue Note years ("Eronel," "Criss Cross"). A potpourri, as it were, a *Best of . . .* , reworked to suit his new quartet—as if, from the pinnacle it had taken him so many years to reach, Monk looked down on his enormous body of work, spread out like a vast plain beneath him. Bird's-eye view, seen through Monk's eye.

From 1962 to 1965, when his initial Columbia contract expired, Monk was put on vinyl no fewer than thirty times. Hard to top that! Every format imaginable: sessions spread over two months just for one album (*Criss Cross*), sessions squeezed into three days, like old times (*Monk*), recording live four days in a row in two different clubs (*Live at the It Club, Live at the Jazz Workshop*), or abroad (*The Tokyo Concerts*), simple anthologies (*Always Know*), big-band pieces (*Big Band and Quartet in Concert*), solo numbers (*Solo Monk*) and of course the quartet. The whole schtick. Columbia had a gold mine and for three years they worked it systematically and avidly. The slogan was, Let the tape roll! Everything's good for a take.

Their enthusiasm was catching: After warming up during most of 1963 with exhaustive tours in Europe and Japan (with a stopover in Honolulu), Monk steamed into 1964 all systems go, with an irresistibly exuberant music. To be perfectly exact, the year actually began on December 30, 1963, at Lincoln Center, which was then vying with Carnegie Hall to present "great musical moments" to the New York elite. And it was a concert with a big band! He kicked off the year in style. What better way to warm up for New Year's Eve? This big band had been reshaped and polished by Monk and Hall Overton since the last concert five years earlier. They not only changed the entire repertoire, but they also shifted the band's center of gravity. They replaced the tuba with a soprano saxophone (Steve Lacy) and doubled the trumpet with a cornet (Thad Jones), which meant that the low register was now only carried by baritone sax and trombone. The emphasis was definitely on the upper register. Deep brassy tones gave way to swaggering stridency. (Had anyone ever written *that* high for soprano sax before? Only a lead player like Lacy could pull it off.) Success at last. This time they did it; they took the time to get it right. This big band was no better or worse than the '59 band; like that one, it was remarkable and excellent. Once again Monk proved that by staying on course and being true to himself, in the end the sheer quality of his music would win the day. Three cheers! Happy New Year, Mr. Monk.

No question, 1964 was the banner year for Thelonious. His entire output from those twelve months is exhilarating, with such energy and fire, one marvels that he could still do it after all that time. True, he had changed musicians. Butch Warren replaced John Ore on bass; in the fall, Warren was replaced by Larry Gales. And then drummer Ben Riley took over for Frankie Dunlop. Dunlop had a sense of swing that was both powerful and intelligent, ideal for both big band and quartet. But Riley was more subtle, with a leaner, suppler beat. Monk had always been attuned to the drummers he played with; their style influenced and nourished him. Ben Riley's arrival gave him new wings. Monk was so pleased with his new recruit that on *It's Monk's Time*, their first recording together, he gave the drummer a place of honor, something he had never done before. Two of the six tracks on the album are for solo piano. In each of the other four, Riley has an extended solo, including one on the first track, "Lulu's Back in Town." Quite unusual! Once when Lacy asked Thelonious if he had any general guidelines about playing his pieces, Monk replied tersely—and the answer says a lot about his conception of music—"Make the drummer sound good." And Riley not only sounds good, his playing is so natural it seems to have always been a part of the Thelonious Monk Quartet. Ben was a rejuvenating breath of fresh air for Thelonious, who in turn breathed new energy into his whole ensemble.

Riley has this to say about how he became part of the band: he was playing a club date with another band, and for a month they shared the bill with the Thelonious Monk Quartet. The pianist barely said a word to him the whole time, standard procedure for Thelonious. The gig ended on a Sunday night; the next morning Ben was wakened by the phone. "Mr. Riley, I'm calling from Columbia Records Studios. Mr. Monk would like you at the recording session for his next album." "When's that?" Ben asked, bewildered. "Why, right now," was the answer. At the time, the drummer had a friend who loved to pull telephone stunts like this. He muttered something and hung up. A second later the phone rang again. "Mr. Riley, I'm *really* calling from Columbia and we need you *now*!"

Riley threw on his clothes, packed up his drums, and raced to the studio where, indeed, the band was waiting for him. He set up his drums; Monk didn't say a word. When Riley was ready, Monk, still silent, launched into the first number. Same routine throughout the session, and the others that followed.

On the last day, Monk came up to him and said, "Did you get paid, at least?" Ben stammered, "Yes. . . . No. . . . It doesn't matter . . ." Monk cut him short: "Good. I like the men in my band to be paid right." Ben gasped. "You mean I'm in the band?" Monk came back with, "Got a passport?" "Uh . . . No, actually . . ." "Well, go and get one. We're going on tour at the end of the week!"

Sure enough, a week later they landed in Amsterdam. Monk was probably somewhere between London and Marseille when the February 28 issue of *Time* magazine hit the stands, with his face on the cover, painted by Chaliapin's son. The cover of *Time*! Him, a jazzman! A black jazzman! Now the only thing missing was a statue on Times Square! Long-feature article: Thelonious Monk, his life, his work. It caused quite a stir, and discussed his bouts with drugs and insanity, along with his music and his career. An in-depth piece, which treated this extraordinary, complex, authentic artist with humor but respect.

You can appreciate the irony of the situation when

you realize that the whole country was still in mourning for John F. Kennedy, assassinated only four months earlier and already quasi-beatified. Because of this national tragedy, both the Lincoln Center concert (originally scheduled for November 1963) and the *Time* cover story had been postponed. But Thelonious shrugged it off. So what? Once again, he was out of sync with the rest of the world. But this time, through a typically Monkish quirk of fate, he was vying for center stage with the President of the United States. No wonder the Columbia people titled his then current record *It's Monk's Time*.

And Monk's time it was. Everyone in Europe knew it, and everywhere he played, houses were packed with his worshiping fans. These concerts were often recorded, usually by national radio, and still turn up on various labels. Every one of them shows that the band had never sounded better. Spring turned into summer. The quartet, with Butch Warren on bass, played the jazz festivals which were starting to take place all over the U.S. The first one was held at Newport in 1955, the brainchild of pianist/promoter/business genius George Wein. The idea took hold and spread—and Monk was a must on every bill. The quartet even played in Pittsburgh, to an audience of thirteen thousand! . . . The Village Gate, the Village Vanguard . . . In June, another big band concert, this time at Carnegie Hall. Autumn: Larry Gales took over on bass and was integrated into what would become the quintessential Thelonious Monk Quartet. They recorded a superb album called simply *Monk* in three days, then took off to tour the West Coast.

With this new band, Thelonious seemed to have rediscovered his taste for taking chances. Monk, tired? The old man's past it? Not a chance! He dredged up tunes from the past you'd have thought were permanently buried in old Prestige or Blue Note catalogs. He even pulled out tunes recorded for Gigi Gryce nine years earlier, when he was at the peak of his creativity. Two of them, "Shuffle Boil" and "Brake's Sake," resurfaced when Ben Riley walked into the Columbia studio. The third, "Gallop's Gallop," was recorded for Columbia live in concert at the It Club. It all swings, it all stays strong, it's all great (except for maybe "Gallop's Gallop," which Rouse doesn't seem to remember too well). For me, 1964 has a tempo. Some years have a smell, others a color or a sound, but I'm sure that for Thelonious, that year had a tempo.

It falls somewhere between 140 and 160 beats a minute. That magic tempo is what every tune on *It's Monk's Time* naturally requires. They all fall into that bracket. Relaxed but fast, a deceptive tempo, allegro ma non troppo. It sounds as if it could go on all day, but it takes the endurance of a marathon runner to keep it up for very long. Monk used to say sarcastically that drummers only knew three tempos: slow, medium, and fast. It seems to me that the year 1964 was spent in constantly exploring a fourth tempo, medium-fast, so perfectly suited to Monk's music. It gives an impression of comfort and speed at the same time. Push the metronome to 180 and you lose this feeling of offhand, nonchalant elegance and edge into a tauter, more restless tempo. Slow it to 120 and you fall right into the medium tempos, which is another sound entirely.

One-forty to 160, that's where it all happens. You pull out of medium and head toward fast. Where will it settle? Somewhere between 140 and 160. Yes, but where? Monk was always interested in this gray area in music where things almost seem to decide by themselves. Listen to his "rubbed-together" melody notes—two notes a half-tone apart and played at the same time, so the ear can't really figure out which one is the melody. Listen to his chords which contain within themselves both harmonic tension and its resolution. Listen to his rhythm, always hovering between an eighth note and a dotted eighth. And listen to his sudden, unexpected silences in the middle of a solo. Even while showing us he's in full control, he loves to plant that seed of doubt, send an idea soaring, let it hang in midair. . . . He suspends time, stretches it out. . . . Monk's time. . . . Will he leave it to our ears to resolve it? Then the axe falls; and after having put it in extreme danger, Monk redefines density with a touch of the finger.

And playing this game at 150 is high art! The ultimate unstable tempo; between liquid and gas: extremely volatile. And yet, that impression of utter ease . . . of palpable existence . . . A whole year of that— what stamina! The whole band turned it on and kept the speedometer right on 150. Highway time! On tour nine months of the year, they maintained their steady cruising speed. Larry Gales had plenty of humor and, in his own inimitable way, played lines which were as mischievous as they were precise—as if he borrowed Monk's trick of leaving harmonic and rhythmic tensions unresolved till the last possible minute. Gales beat around the bush. He'd go off the beat, then on it, then back off it, then loop around it, for bars at a time. Zigzagging, taking detours, anticipating well in advance where he would finally end up. And all in subtle shades. Nothing obvious. What counted above all was the beat. He didn't pull anything fast, except the rhythm! When it was time for his solo, then he'd let himself go and, with a tip of his hat to Duke Ellington, turn a simple idea over and over with the patience of a cat playing with a mouse, and squeeze every ounce of resonance from his instrument.

And when his solo was over and he merged back into the rhythm section, he would turn to Ben Riley, his colleague. Between 1964 and 1968, those two put in a lot of mileage together. Instruments often had to be rented on the spot, the sound systems were sometimes a disaster . . . Trains, buses, planes, and ships. And every night only one dictum: Give the tunes the right sound, and keep the beat. If they gave out frequent-flyer bonuses for number of hours spent keeping the beat, they would have won a lot of free trips. Or a place in jazz heaven. Or both. Riley's musical creed was simple and effective: The less you put in, the better it sounds. He pretty much stuck to the basic drum set : bass drum, snare, cymbal, and high hat. One for each limb. He used the rest only when he really had to. He could get twenty different sounds from his snare drum alone, from a gentle whisper of his brushes to an explosion in combination with the bass drum. In between the two, he had a huge range of strokes, which he played with care and precision to make the skin sing. Less is more. It's a well-known fact. He played accents and syncopation with taste, restraint, and subtlety. After all, he had to walk with the bass and at the same time fly with Thelonious. Being Monk's drummer wasn't an easy task: Some, like Blakey, matched egos with him, in a kind of summit meeting. Others chose to "boost" his music by adding their own energy and intelligence, such as Frankie Dunlop. But Riley tried the impossible: to fade into the background and still make his presence felt. That was his solution—there when you needed him, but never in the way. Shadow Wilson was like that, too. It took a lot of tact, a lot of humility, and most of all, a real love for Monk's music.

Gales the mischievous and Riley the discreet. Thelonious had found two disciples devoted to his cause, each of whom highlighted a facet of his own genius. And let's not forget Charlie Rouse, who seemed to live inside the music. Add him to the mix and you have a perfectly balanced quartet: small wonder it held the record for longevity. This cohesion was severely tested, for the band was almost constantly on the road. From 1964 to 1968, they did four European tours, one in Australia (a flop), and one in Japan. And those were just the overseas tours, without even mentioning the countless North American tours and all the club dates, which were much easier to organize. When they were on the road, their gigs were mostly one-nighters, every day a different city, even a different country. To pick one at random, here's the itinerary for their European tour in March 1965.

1965—March	3	Stockholm
	7	Paris
	8	Bremen
	9	Cologne
	10	Mainz
	12	Scheveningen
	13	Amsterdam
	14	London
	17	Birmingham
	18	Manchester
	21	San Remo

Then, with no break at all, on to Australia, immediately followed by a month on the West Coast, since it was on the way home. Nonstop concerts from February 26 to May 16. A typical day on the road: eight A.M., wake-up call. Bus to the airport. Eleven A.M., takeoff.

One P.M., land at destination. Bus, hotel, press conference. Nap. Five P.M., soundcheck at the concert venue. contact with the local inhabitants who are all very friendly and admiring, but who speak a funny language. Seven P.M., dinner. Ten P.M., concert, if there happens to be a warm-up band. And then it's play, play, and play some more. Midnight, the final encore. Wind down, have a few drinks, eat, hang out. To bed around two or three A.M. And then it starts all over again. Three months of it. Exhausting.

And when each member of the quartet knows by heart *every* figure and *every* phrase of the other three, it takes enormous solidarity to hold things together for four years. Discouragement, depression, getting fed up, losing faith—strictly forbidden. Music, music, and more music! Shotgun marriage! Burning desire! Ordeal by fire!

And what's more, the contract with Columbia Records was about to expire. Should they renew it? Obviously. But on what terms? It was Monk's shining hour; his name was praised in every language. But a company like Columbia had to be "accountable to its shareholders," as the expression goes. Behind a door marked Business Affairs sat an accountant who added up the columns. Monk: credits, debits. . . . We recorded him a lot these last three years. Sales can't keep up. Poor production: yield ratio. I can imagine a phone call to Macero: No more money; hold everything; one album a year. Word became deed. In three years, three albums, eight recording dates total. Plus a Brubeck-Monk duo recorded live in Mexico City (under Brubeck's name), the time it would take to do an Ellington blues. And I imagine Monk's advance when the contract was renewed was revised downward. His label was letting him down. Thanks, pal, but we're looking for something more contemporary. How about putting an electric guitar in your band?

This was tough. They made it clear to him that he'd been around a little too long. Not exactly reassuring. Jazz artists who survived the big cut in the fifties did it by evolving. Miles, Dizzy, Rollins, they all got into electric music at the end of the following decade. They moved with the times. But Monk's time is different from that of all the others. He wasn't contemporary, and he wasn't traditional. He was Monk. Which is precisely why his music lasted, and will go on lasting as long as people have ears. And it will still resurface two, ten, twenty generations from now. Even extraterrestrials will hear it.

But the people at Columbia had their sights set on the immediate future, and what they saw was that they wouldn't be able to milk the Monk cow much longer. They couldn't wait twenty years for his comeback . . . there were the shareholders to think about . . . and he had made plenty of records, all of them good. If they were going to be able to sell the next one, it would really have to be something newer and fresher than the others.

And yet, his first two recordings under the new contract, *Straight, No Chaser* and *Underground*, proved that his creative fountain was still flowing. All the tempos are played with superb elegance. For *Underground*, Monk came up with no less than four new numbers; one, "Ugly Beauty," is a waltz, the first in fifty years. He even wrote a tune for his daughter, who was there in the studio—the ambiguous and delicious "Boo Boo's Birthday." Plus "Thelonious," the first trio number he had recorded since his early days at Riverside, eleven years earlier. Both albums reveal a maturity and a striking sense of confidence. From 1965 to 1967, he crisscrossed Europe, Japan and of course the U.S. He put his big band together for a European tour and it was once again a huge success. He even took part in an "all-star" band called the Bop Fathers, with Dizzy Gillespie, James Moody, Milt Jackson, Percy Heath, and Max Roach, all his old friends. Unfortunately, no recordings remain from this American tour, but by all accounts the music was everything you'd expect from such a group of greats.

So Monk had two irons in the fire: a label, though their support seemed to be dwindling, and a band, who'd been all over the planet with him since 1961. And that was just the trouble. At that pace, soon everyone in the world would have heard him. There weren't many place left on the jazz circuit that hadn't already featured him. Columbia's predictions were about to come true: through overexposure, he would soon be out of style. If *Who's Who* wanted a seven-line biography of Monk, this is what I'd propose:

1. 1917–27: Birth of a genius
2. 1927–37: Childhood of a genius
3. 1937–47: Apprenticeship
4. 1947–57: Ascension
5. 1957–67: Glory
6. 1967–77: Decline
7. 1977–82: Silence

You get the point. Monk had reached saturation point. The wheel was turning. The big crowds no longer flocked to hear jazz; now they wanted rock, pop, the Beatles, things that sold twenty times better. The age of marketing had come. The days when a few black rebels reinvented music and dignity at Minton's Playhouse were long gone. You have to sell, man; change your style, get with it; jazz isn't *in* anymore. And the supreme irony:

Underground won a Grammy, not for its content, which was excellent, but for its cover design. What counts is the front; it's all in the packaging. Monk honored for his record cover! (Which is magnificent, by the way.) Oh, he still played, but in ever-less suitable settings: stadiums, arenas, for celebrations, in ridiculous, enormous places. The seventies were coming up, when they did things big. Monk was now becoming part of the furniture. The up-and-coming piano players were young terrors like Herbie Hancock, McCoy Tyner, and Chick Corea. Jazz-rock was simmering on the back burner, and music was on the brink of changing very quickly.

Columbia went with the tide and for Monk's last album with them, they requested not quite that he play electric piano, but that he record with a big band. Not Hall Overton's this time; something new was needed. Their idea was to take Monk's biggest hits and have them arranged by a jazz orchestrator whose album *More Blues and the Abstract Truth* showed that he had a feel for economy in music. He had moved to L.A. in 1967 and was writing for movies and TV. He was the ideal candidate for adding "dimension" to Monk's music. An experienced jazzman, he nevertheless knew all the arranger's tricks for making his work salable to all audiences. This was Oliver Nelson. The intention was honorable enough, though it left a bitter aftertaste. Monk revamped into TV theme music; what would they think of next?

Nelson took Monk's compositions and gave them a California sheen. A syrupy glaze, with hot fudge sauce, crushed nuts, and whipped cream. All the thorns of the *cactus Monkus* were smoothed, polished and filed down. His spare, restrained solos were neatly and efficiently framed by the big band—a highly professional job of plastic surgery. The timeless Beast became the ephemeral Beauty for a night. The result, as you might expect, was totally kitsch. An interesting if predictable turnaround: By trying to modernize Monk, by taking over control of his music, they knocked him off his rightful pedestal, and made him an artist of the day, like hundreds of others, a product which quickly goes out of style.

It was the first time in his long career that Monk had gotten involved in such a dubious enterprise; he'd always avoided such fiascos. Most artists, even the greats, have produced at least one bomb somewhere along the way; a moment of weakness, a lapse of taste. But up until now, Monk never had. For one simple reason: he always played the same way. You can't go wrong with the Monk seal of approval! Then, at age fifty-one, he lowered his guard for a second and the Monkmobile started to skid. Nothing spectacular, the music was still good, but you get the feeling he no longer had such a firm grasp on the wheel. The iron fist relaxed its grip and all at once the road took a curve.

This album, titled with unintentional insight *Monk's Blues*, marked the beginning of the descent; from then on, his music became dispersed. He had exploded in the sixties, and now he was experiencing fallout. Everything was breaking up around him. He left Columbia without signing with another label. Monk was on discount. Larry Gales and Ben Riley quit the band in 1969, to be replaced by a string of successors, none of whom stayed long. In 1970, finally even Rouse walked out, right in the middle of a week's gig at the Village Vanguard (what could have happened that night?) after twelve years of loyal service, the twelve best and most fruitful years of his career. Pat Patrick took his place, soon followed by Paul Jeffrey, who stayed with Monk till the end, with excellent musicianship and touching devotion. But he was from a different generation, and there was so much he hadn't lived through with Thelonious. A page had been turned, and nothing could change that.

Besides, the whole jazz market was falling apart. Sales were plummeting, and there were fewer concerts. The only way out was to go big. Promoter George Wein was the most visionary figure on the scene. His success at Newport led him to organize other jazz festivals, first in other cities, then in other countries, often (even in Tokyo) still called "the Newport Festival." In other words, signing on with Wein meant you had work for six months out of the year. When times got tough in 1971, Wein put together a new band with musicians who were having trouble booking tours for their own bands. He rounded up Kai Winding, Sonny Stitt, Dizzy Gillespie, Al McKibbon, Art Blakey and Thelonious for a one-shot tour and sold them as "the Jazz Giants." And off they went. Twenty-nine concerts from September to November, one every other day: Australia, New Zealand, Japan, Israel, Europe, the United States. Musically, it didn't make much sense. Each man took his turn in the ring: Come one, come all, visit the museum of jazz for only three dollars fifty. Flawless individual performances; six concerts for the price of one.

I once asked pianist Ahmad Jamal why he'd never recorded with Miles Davis, who spoke so highly of him. With a wave of his hand, Jamal dismissed the question as absurd but nonetheless answered succinctly, "Two leaders."

Except in this case there weren't two leaders, but five. For the listener, as you can imagine, the result is pretty mediocre. Monk scrupulously confines himself to the role of accompanist, with remarkable restraint and his usual skill. I have the feeling that Dizzy was the group's unofficial leader. Consummate showman that he was, he was a logical choice to organize this eclectic reunion of artists. But it also draws the band toward the spectacular, the sensational. After all, isn't one of their pieces Dizzy's own "Tour De Force?" On "Tin Tin Deo," the trumpeter even goes so far as to take over on piano for a duo with bassist McKibbon that takes guts, with Monk sitting right there. But Thelonious keeps a low profile. Backing up Kai Winding, he tones down the usual acid bite of his accompaniment, as if he doesn't want to inconvenience this trombonist with whom he has so little in common. Same thing with Sonny Stitt. Sometimes with Dizzy, he gets a little bolder, but it all sounds pretty tame when you know what he is capable of. And when it's his turn to solo, he plays with his usual freedom, but without the antic brilliance so characteristic of his own recordings. The pay was good, he did the job. Blakey was furious at seeing his old friend constantly reduced to the thankless and petty role of accompanist, as if he were being squeezed into a suit that was too tight. He railed against Dizzy, who, out of Monk's huge repertoire, remembered almost nothing but "Round Midnight" and "Epistrophy," whereas the pianist played all the trumpeter's hits by heart. Goerge Wein even confided later that Dizzy was astounded by the ovation that always greeted the first notes of "Blue Monk." Blakey fumed that it was outrageous not to show more respect for the pianist's work, and to play it so badly. Monk had no status. He didn't open his mouth during the whole tour, but sank into a silence that could have been taken for indifference, and was certainly resigned. The muted Monk was going to pieces.

And yet in London, during the band's first stay there, Alan Bates, producer for the English label Black Lion, took advantage of the stroke of luck which had handed him Monk, Blakey and McKibbon, all in one package. August 1951–November 1971: the same trio that had played on Blue Note twenty years earlier. The pianist was no longer under contract with anybody, the drummer would do anything for his buddy, and the bassist went for whatever came along. "Want to come by Chappell Studio this afternoon and record a couple of numbers?" "Sure. What'll we play?" "We'll see."

It didn't look promising—none of the psychological conditions essential to a successful recording clicked: Monk was exhausted. He'd just spent two grueling months on the road with a pickup band that treated his compositions with humiliating indifferece. The studio was packed with journalists, producers, and devoted friends, all trying to add their grain of salt to this historic session. There was virtually no program, and even the few weak suggestions were snubbed by Monk's silence. Don't you want to play something by Jimmy Yancee, Thelonious? And what about "Criss Cross"? You don't want to do "Criss Cross"? How about a blues? A recording session should be a private affair, so it must have been unnerving to have everyone carrying on behind the glass partition separating the band from the sound engineer. What were they getting all excited about? And why were they all looking at him like that? As if he were a monkey in a cage.

Furthermore, Al McKibbon was embarassed because it had been twenty years since he'd played Monk's repertoire; since then, there'd been a lot of new material, and not the sort of stuff that can be picked up in a minute. Blakey and Thelonious shared the same view of the situation, except, unlike Monk, Blakey talked about it. And when he did, it was in very strong terms. But he was also aware that this session was special and had an unhoped-for quality: It was the last chance to record with his buddy, before Monk clammed up for good . . . and he knew that Monk wasn't far from it. You can feel that kind of thing when you're on the road with someone, and Blakey was trying to do his best. . . . Everyone was under pressure . . . What would happen? . . . Would Thelonious come through?

You bet he did! And with flying colors! Well, maybe a little rusty . . . After all, he'd been an "entertainer" for the past two months, but he stayed on course and pulled it together—as usual, in pure Monk style. Be prepared, that was his motto. Monk was born ready. The years 1941, '51, '61, '71—it was always the same. In three hours he recorded thirteen solo pieces, and in the next three hours, another nine pieces with his trio. In six hours' studio time, the equivalent of three CDs. Quite a feat! Just like the old days. Blakey immediately fell back in sync with the pianist, and even if he did mess up on a couple of details (they hadn't recorded together since 1958), he proved on this occasion that he had the rare gift of even making a mistake sound good. McKibbon followed suit, sometimes with a blind confidence. (Certain solo versions were, in fact, opportunities for the bassist to practice the changes. On "Crepuscule with Nellie," you can hear McKibbon way in the background trying to pick up the bass notes by ear.) . . . But it didn't matter because Monk was in charge. As long as they took the trouble to play his music the way he wanted it, he delivered his message with clarity and steadfast conviction. Loud and clear.

Bates had the good sense to let the tape roll from the moment Monk entered the studio. And you can hear

Monk, on the tune so cleverly titled "Chordially," trying things out on the piano he discovers in the studio. It's amazing. He is constantly looking for colors, sounds, and phrases. He can't help it. He doesn't play warm-up excercises, but immediately strikes up a rapport with his instrument. He makes the piano speak the music right away. But at the same time, he is searching: at the age of fifty-four, he is still getting new sounds from the keyboard. A piano . . . What is it? How does it work? Do you think it's loaded? If I hit this key, what does that do? Monk extracts lush, rich chords from this big old box, out of which halting yet vigorous melodies seem to rise by themselves. Twenty times you think, He will go into one of his many compositions. Twenty times you think you've recognized a chord progression that reminds you of a song, but instead he continues taking the music farther and farther—*out there*. Thelonious isn't finished yet; if given the chance, he still has some tricks up his sleeve, and a few things cooking on a back burner.

Except for the rare occasion, there wouldn't be another chance. This album is Monk's last will and testament. He turns his attention to the past—to his younger years. "Criss Cross," recorded twenty years before with the same trio; "Evidence," "Misterioso," "Ruby, My Dear," from the Prestige years, the same old stuff reexamined with a young man's confidence. The standards, the compositions, he digs down deep into his memory for what must seem to him most worthy of posterity. Thelonious knew what he was doing. He witnessed his life growing dark and he knew that there would be only rare glimpses of light penetrating into the dim cellars of his silence. This session hasn't aged in the least. Monk could not have better completed his own discography.

His one consolation in these dark years was his son, who was twenty-one in 1970. He played drums, and showed some interest in his father's music. Tootie recalls that at the time the hip thing was to build your own stereo speakers. As a typical rock 'n' roll handyman, he built one enormous speaker that he wanted to test with his own records. At that time, he wasn't fully conscious of the genius of Thelonious Sr., whom he took for granted without fully understanding it. Rather than risk blowing out his speaker with a Jimi Hendrix album, he chose an older record from his father's collection off the Prestige label, certain that such a mild recording couldn't possibly harm his new system. So he put the album on the turntable and glued his ear to the speaker to get the full effect of the sound. What a shock! He had put on "Work"—one of Monk's wildest compositions! He was stunned. The hell with the system, he turned up the volume and played the tune over and over two, five, ten times. The truth dawned on him: His father was undeniably a genius.

In light of this experience, he now understood why the critics took so much time to appreciate the beauty of his father's music. You have to really *listen* in order to get it. After all, hadn't it taken him twenty-one years to understand it? And a week later, as if by chance, Thelonious asked his son, "Are you ready?" Junior understood and didn't hesitate. Two days later, the new quartet recorded a tevevision show for a national network. The year was 1970 and although Tootie didn't leave for Japan that year with the quartet, he would be part of the regular group from 1971 . . . until the end.

The end. You could feel it coming. More and more often, Monk was "ill." A second tour with the Jazz Giants in 1972 was to be his final circuit before he went into retirement, from which he would only emerge on rare occasions. His friends were anxious and saddened by his silence, and they continued to play his music even in his absence. In April 1974, Tootie, Paul Jeffrey, and Barry Harris organized a concert featuring a host of impressive musicians, in honor of Thelonious. His music had been arranged for brass and strings, and it was an ambitious project. Would Thelonoius come? No one was counting on it. And then, a few seconds before the concert began, the curtain moved, a head appeared. It was Monk! Hurray! Barry Harris, ecstatic at the sight of him, turned the keyboard over to the Master who, with a sure hand, once again inspired the entire band to a dazzling performance!

Then in July 1975, he broke his silence to present his quartet—comprised of his son, Paul Jeffrey, and Larry Ridley—at Philharmonic Hall (today Avery Fisher Hall). They were to play the last set of a full night of music, featuring the up-and-coming group Oregon, as well as a new piano star named Keith Jarrett. Oregon was a roaring success. Break. Keith Jarrett came on, raised the piano top and, with great care, repositioned the mikes above the instrument. He played particularly well. The crowd went wild. Break. Tootie later admitted that sitting through these preliminary sets, he had dreaded having to stand by helplessly, watching his father be sacrificed in the name of youth and change. How could an old-timer like Monk be able to win over such an obviously modern audience? The sound engineer, after his experience with Jarrett, leaned over and asked Monk how he wanted the mikes placed. Offhandedly, the pianist pointed to his instrument, raised an eyebrow, and said, "Well, over the piano, I guess. . . ."

Then the curtain went up . . . hearts stopped . . . and in a few bars, Monk erased all the music that had preceded him. Oregon, Jarrett, the microphones, the public, the rumors, the solitude, time itself—he blew them all away. The new music, modernism, the handsome piano, new dimensions—vanished. Monk's music spoke the truth. "I mean you," "Ba-lue Bolivar Ba-lues-Are Ba-lue," "We see," Misterioso" . . . "Round Midnight.". . . Thelonious Monk, the genius of modern music. And the audience knew it and gave him an overwhelming ovation that seemed to go on forever. The crowd was delirious. His genius was intact, for all to acclaim.

He returned to Carnegie Hall in March and again in June 1976 with the same rhythm section, the same sax player, plus trumpeter Lonnie Hillyer, and, so it seems, with guitarist Rodney Jones. Nothing was recorded; there was simply a concert review by longtime admirer Ira Gitler who, not surprisingly, described Thelonious as unshakable, at the top of his form, sharp as ever, forever young and always good. And then came the end. In the late 1970s, a prostrate operation, followed by bladder surgery, compelled him to use a catheter and a humiliating bag. Most of the time he would answer in monosyllables when his friends called. No, he didn't want to see them again. No, he didn't want to play with his old buddies from the great days of bebop. No, he had no desire to play at all anymore. No, he didn't even want to go out to the clubs to hear them play. No, he no longer played the piano. No. No. No.

Curtains.

‖ 12 ‖

Fade to Black

Monk's final silence remains an enigma. The pianist progressively withdrew from the world. Then, quite simply, he no longer existed. Fade to black. Oh, people knew he was still alive. Rumor had it that he was in Weehawken, at Pannonica's, but he no longer ventured out, and the few relentless friends who called him would often receive only a succinct groan on the end of the line. It has often been said that Monk's famous musical silences ended up taking over his life at the end. That he had pushed himself "to the very limits of his system" and finally disappeared into nothingness. His personal silence has often been linked to his sparse musical style. As if, in a sort of Archimedes principle of communicating vessels, he paid with his life for the uniqueness of his art. Was he silent, as some have said, because he had nothing else to say? Did he have so little to say before? Is that the meaning of the silence in his music? And yet many other artists used silence—Jamal, Miles, Basie—and they didn't spend their last years in deliberate isolation. . . .

Monk had two types of silence: the silence of the man who observed what was happening around him, and the silence of the musician who created music. They are very different: one is subjected to time, and the other *creates* time. No—if there was a mystical connection between the end of Monk's life and his music, I see it more in his relationship with *form*. Earlier on, we saw how little he was concerned with form, as if it were a necessity of a second order. It was always the case in his band that solos followed one after the other as long as there were musicians there to improvise. Once the whole band had soloed, the melody was played one last time. In this simple and classic structure, there were no unpleasant surprises. But as Thelonious got older, he would sometimes end his solos ambiguously. For most of his contemporaries, the end of a solo was a kind of punctuation which they made it a point of honor to play with the greatest clarity and conviction. In so doing, they were sending a clear message: I've spoken. Next. However, Monk, in his brilliant indifference to form, adopted the habit of finishing his solos with fewer and fewer phrases. Was he going to turn it over to the next soloist? Had he truly said everything? . . . Yes? . . . No—for there he was, continuing to play. No one knew exactly what to do. He was no longer really playing phrases. Technically speaking, they were chords. At times, two notes stood out, a promise of the next player, but no, he continued to unravel more and more—was it the end yet? What were you supposed to do there in the middle of the chord progression? A solo is supposed to begin at the beginning of the form, not in the middle.

In his music as in his life, Thelonious was informal. It was true in the ordinary sense of someone who didn't burden himself with social conventions, but also in the profound sense of a man who structured his life differently from others. It is generally understood that he didn't make a career; rather, the world clung to his genius for ten years. And when his popularity waned, he never tried to maintain a small circuit of festivals which would have provided him with a certain amount of security in his old age—as if his ten years of glory had been a long and wonderful solo that ended along with the 1960s. By making fewer and fewer appearances, he made way for new improvisers. But even then, form remained unclear, and for a long time those in the jazz world continued to believe in the prophet's return. The famous Carnegie Hall concert in 1974, where Monk suddenly materialized before a jubilant Barry Harris, was proof enough. Only when he dropped out of sight for good, did we realize Monk had played his last solo.

But the question remains: Why did he stop? Why didn't he go on for another fifteen, twenty years? He'd spent half his life fighting for recognition, so why did he quit when he had finally made it? A musician is a musician for life. He doesn't quit halfway. Great jazzmen play to the end, and they die with their boots on—or, like Molière, die right onstage. That is their tradition.

Miles had flirted with this paradox and, jaded by it all, shut himself away for several years. Rollins had also stopped everything in his quest for wisdom. But they each had reappeared from the shadows to proclaim, in a new and stronger voice, their imperious desire to play. It has to come out, or life becomes unbearable. Freud once wrote that an artist is a neurotic who treats himself.

I believe that a musician is the perfect example of this basic truth. Even when shut away in a dismal cell of a New York psychiatric hospital, Bud Powell drew a piano keyboard on the wall, on which he played in silence. But in Monk's case, it seemed to go beyond self-medication . . . no one knows exactly where the cause—or the effect—was. It was all one huge impervious block.

Thelonious had always been strange. Friends who knew him well say that he had a logic all his own. Others insist that he wasn't crazy at all, and that he only behaved that way in order to give himself an image; then, as he got older, he became trapped in his own game. Yet there always seems to be something quite troubling. Underlying all these statements, there seems to be something very troubling, which Monk's apparent nonchalance was unable to hide, because from time to time, Monk truly took leave of his senses. His little dance steps and incongruous remarks would give way to feverish intensity. He would pace back and forth in a room, for hours on end. He wouldn't utter a word for three whole days, and would remain standing without sleeping, all the while grinding his teeth. Then, he would collapse like a felled oak tree, and remain in bed for two days straight. . . . His gaze became vacant, as if he were held prisoner by an evil force which was gnawing at him, destroying him, of which he was unable to speak. He could sit for eight hours in a row without moving a muscle. . . . Or, in a strange city, he would walk for miles, until he reached open country, where he'd be picked up by a police patrol car.

Yes, Monk was mad. He suffered from attacks. He was sick and he knew it. And he could feel the rising wave as it started to overtake him, then carried him far away from the world of other people. The strange, endearing character suddenly turned into a frightening creature. A dark shroud seemed to rise from the depths of his soul and enfold his entire being in its pall. In a matter of hours, he cut all bonds with the real world one by one, and isolated himself, against his will, in a fortress whose walls grew thicker by the minute. Mad. Monk was mad.

He had, as the saying goes, a medical record. The first documented instance dates back to 1959. I do not know whether he spent time in psychiatric hospitals before this date. He probably did, although Thelonious was very careful: during the 1950s he rarely left New York, which served literally as his safeguard. And under the affectionate care of Nellie and those close to him, Monk was immediately brought back to the house in case of a problem. An accident was likely to happen only if he was away from home, by himself, and subject to one of his "attacks." That's exactly what happened in '59.

Hired to play in Boston at George Wein's club, the Storyville, Monk left Nellie behind and took the train up by himself. During the trip, the all-too-familiar dark shroud began to appear. When he arrived, he went straight to his hotel, only slightly behind schedule. In the lobby, he went into a spinning dance, then stopped abruptly and began staring fixedly at something in the room, ignoring the manager's injunctions. That distinguished gentleman then told him, in no uncertain terms, that there was no room in the hotel for him. So, without a word, Monk went to the club where his fans and an anxious boss awaited him, locked himself in his dressing room and began staring at the wall without moving. When he finally decided to go onstage, he performed two numbers and then, to everyone's amazement, stood up and left the club. An hour later, he returned, played two more numbers, then lapsed into a state of prostration from which nothing could shake him. The hypnotized audience fell silent and waited. Time went by. His embarrassed accompanists walked off the stage, leaving him alone at the piano. More time went by. Amidst the sepulchral silence, he got up and left the club once and for all. He made his way to the airport, where he wandered around, lost in a daze. The airport police were notified, and when they spotted him, they knew they were dealing with a deranged individual. His massive form and menacing silence seemed to be a danger to both himself and to others. He was immediately taken to the hospital.

He was one of the many people who wander aimlessly through airports or train stations, as if they cherished the vain hope of a voyage by which they coud flee themselves and soothe their pain. This is a common occurrence, and the police know how to handle such cases. Routine procedure is to direct the sick person, with every necessary precaution, to a psychiatric hospital. On arrival, the case is explained to the intern on duty, who questions the patient, sometimes without a word in response. Then the intern points to a wing of the hospital reserved for such patients and sighs: schizophrenic.

Monk remained in the Boston hospital for several days before Nellie, who was worried sick, was finally informed by one of their friends. This time it was serious. Monk had attained fame and recognition, offers were pouring in, and his friends and loved ones were thrilled to see the positive turn his life seemed to be taking . . . but at the same time, at regular intervals, he would crack completely. His fits of madness were becoming more and more serious. He suffered at least two a year, and then the frequency and the length of these dark periods increased.

Inevitably, it is tempting to draw up a psychiatric profile of Thelonious Monk. The process is not new. Scores of psychohistorians have tried to categorize the great artists of the past into various types. Signs of epilepsy were identified in both Van Gogh and Flaubert; Balzac was said to have been manic-depressive, Bartók autistic, and Mozart was thought to have suffered from Tourette's syndrome. But, obviously, such classifications can be arbitrary and approximate. Each case is unique and obstinately resists any form of generalization. Some symptoms are known, but so many others remain obscure. These illnesses can only be studied in clinical conditions over a long period of time, and even then, the results are inconclusive. So it is very difficult to give a diagnosis without ever having met the man in question.

Thelonious was very discreet on the subject. When the Boston incident became known, he treated it with characteristic evasiveness: "People say I'm crazy. It's not true. Sure, I was in there, but they let me out. . . ."

His sense of humor continued to mask a reality which consisted of more frequent hospital "rest cures" and visits from doctors. From the age of sixty-five, his withdrawal periods of several weeks, or even months, began to interrupt his lengthy world tours. People knew that Monk was getting needed rest, and that he wasn't well.

Trumpet player Eddie Henderson was an intern at UCLA's Langley Porter Psychiatric Institute in San Francisco in mid-1969 when Thelonious arrived at the hospital accompanied by Nellie. Monk was performing at the Both Ends Club. Eddie's testimony is precise and professional, and gives us excellent insight into the psychiatric procedures of that period, as well as Monk's part in them.

When they brought him to the hospital, Monk was

wrapped up in his overcoat in a near-catatonic state. His only perceptible movements were his eyes, the grinding of his teeth, and the hand on which he wore his famous ring, as he turned it fist-up. From time to time he would break his silence to mutter, "Monk know, Monk know," then sink back into silence. He was put through all the standard tests (the Rorschach test, thematic apperception test) with no reaction on his part. The problem was that he suffered from deep inner turmoil. Consequently, the doctors had to advance to the next stage—administering neuroleptics to the patient which were supposed to provide relief. And this is where Henderson stepped in. Of all the doctors on duty, he was the only one who had heard of Monk. He knew about the disastrous effect of a wrong dosage on a patient. He also assumed that Thelonious used narcotics to some extent and offered to take responsibility for him. According to Eddie, the most widely used neuroleptic at the time was Thorazine. The minimum dosage was 50 milligrams and its effect, theoretically, was to "pacify" the patient for approximately twelve hours. As this dosage proved ineffective on Thelonious, it was gradually increased and in a few days time, reached 3500 milligrams! Seventy times the initial dosage! Thirty-five hundred is the maximum dosage, beyond which the patient's life is endangered. But Thelonious came to see him again grinding his teeth: "Hey, Doc! I can't sleep. . . . Can't you give me a little more?"

Monk was allowed to perform in town on the condition that the trumpeter become his chaperone for the week. One night he arrived at the club with the three and a half grams of Thorazine coursing through his system. He went up to the bar, ordered a triple cognac, drained the glass, and proceeded to his dressing room. There he snorted a gram of coke, kindly provided by an admiring fan, before going onstage. Which takes us back to the scene I described earlier: Monk seated at the piano, sweating profusely and pressing the keys down without producing the least sound. During the break, he went back to the bar where Eddie was sitting and said through his teeth, "Good set, huh?"

Each night the doctor would take Thelonious back to the hospital. As his condition wasn't improving, he was given an EEG. The reading didn't point to any solution, but seemed to indicate a heavy absorption of various drugs over a long period. The consultant performed the next operation recommended for certain schizophrenic cases: electroshock therapy. The aim of this extremely violent procedure was to artifically trigger an epileptic fit from which the patient would emerge feeling better. The electrodes were placed on Thelonious and they gave him the juice.

Thelonious didn't move. In fact, he became more rigid than ever, as if that cruel stimulation increased his resistance to treatment. He ground his teeth. Eddie said, "Stop!" If they went any further, they'd kill him.

Monk remained in the hospital for a month. His condition subsided and once again he was in a "normal" state. His perception of reality, as illustrated by his constant oblique remarks, indicated an alert and functioning individual. According to the American medical establishment, Monk suffered from "unclassified schizophrenia" and, since his behavior didn't seem to be dangerous, he was released into the custody of his wife, who brought him back to New York.

The noose was getting tighter. In the late 1960s, Nellie and Monk left their apartment on 63rd Street and moved into larger quarters in a modern building a few blocks away. Then, in 1973, Pannonica offered the couple the top floor of her stately home in New Jersey. Nellie, exhausted from years of constant caring for her husband, graciously accepted. They retreated into this secluded estate as into a castle stronghold with a drawbridge. And there, sheltered from the stares and intrusions of the outside world, Thelonious began his long descent into the dungeon of his distress.

Monk was being picked up in airports. He had a "family history"; and his father was suspected of having suffered from mental problems. His attacks seemed to have begun relatively late in life, from about the age of twenty-seven, and occurred with regularity. He never served in the military. Confronted with such a medical file and the above description, a psychiatrist today could classify Monk as a hebephrenic, since his schizophrenia didn't produce any perceptible delirium (hallucinations, voices), but seemed to be negative, and accompanied by symptoms of withdrawal and apathy. Moreover, hebephrenia is known to be the state which precedes autism. This would provide one explanation for his final silence, one way of rationalizing it without fully understanding it.

Also, Monk's massive consumption of drugs made diagnosis even more difficult. He had been taking drugs indiscriminately for a long time—tranquilizers, cocaine, alcohol, speed (which would account for his staying awake for three days at a time, followed by a total collapse), and, most likely, acid, even if he was a little old for that. I can't picture him as a heroin addict, with the spoon, the works, and the rubber band, but he must have snorted some when it was passed around . . . and mixed it with all the rest. Thelonious was not a one-drug man.

He had such a strong constitution he could tolerate mixtures which would kill an ox. The least we can say is that drugs did get him into serious trouble.

In the pseudo-liberal and inevitably racist society of New York in the 1940s, drugs provided any cops who had a grudge against blacks or jazz musicians with the perfect pretext for making their lives miserable. Although legislation was incapable of curbing the endemic development of organized crime, it did have one useful provision for this type of case, aside from prison: the famous "cabaret card." One wrong move by a musician and his card could be revoked. He was then banned from performing in the city for a period of time to be determined by a judge. This was a simple and practical system—you just had to catch a jazz musician with a little dope on him. Doctors, lawyers, movie stars, businessmen, and politicians, all had their secret shelf of substances which could open doors to heightened pleasures or parallel lives. But for the musician, that would be too easy.

As early as 1948, Thelonious was arrested for possession of a marijuana joint. His card was revoked for a month. So it's not surprising that we can't account for his time during that period. Then, three years later, in 1951, he was struck by a harder blow. Reports relating to this incident differ and, aside from the officer who made the arrest, those involved were evasive about it. What seems certain is that Bud and Monk were motioned to pull their car over. When the officer approached them, Thelonious apparently threw a bag of heroin out of the window to avoid getting caught with it. Only a month earlier, Bud had had a run-in with a female undercover agent who had implored him to sell her a joint in order to arrest him for drug trafficking. So this petty little performance now seemed more like a setup than anything else.

In any case, this incident resulted in a two-month sentence. Two solid months! Knowing Thelonious, you can imagine the state of depression he must have been in. He had a wife and child, a career that he had been trying earnestly to build, and now he was labeled as a criminal, a threat to society, and was put away. And when he got out, his cabaret card was revoked for nearly six years, as he was a second offender. He was barred from performing in the city and from earning his livelihood. Nothing serious, Mr. Monk; surely you can find a job as a night watchman or an elevator operator, which would be more appropriate to a man of your social condition. Give up these pipe dreams of being a jazz musician and resume the place in society which you never should have left.

Nineteen-fifty-one–fifty-seven: The end of his Blue Note contract, his whole adventure with Prestige, and a third of his work for Riverside. During this entire period, Thelonious was condemned to silence. Barred from playing in public.

And that's not all: in the fall of '58, a year after his card was reissued, Monk, Rouse, and the Baroness were on their way to Philadelphia. They stopped in a small Delaware town where Thelonious got out of the Bentley to get a drink at a motel. But in Delaware, the sight of a big, silent black man was frightening. They didn't like having blacks in the neighborhood to begin with. So what happened? Someone called the police, of course, and when they arrived, they found Monk at the wheel of a Bentley. Blacks don't drive Bentleys. You get the picture. . . . "Chief, I got one here in a stolen car! Hurry up, he looks like trouble. Handcuff him—let him have it: Resisting arrest. What's in the car? Well, if it isn't marijuana! Lock him up!" All that for a drink. And the verdict: a two-month sentence and a two-year suspension of the cabaret card. This was going too far. This time, however, the Baroness was with him. She had influence and social standing—just what jazz musicians lacked. Her lawyers quickly demolished the charges against Thelonious. Four months later, the case was dismissed. This was a close call and the only thing that saved him was the fact that now, because of his connections and his prestige as a musician, he was too big a fish for a small-time cop.

Admittedly, though, drugs printed an indelible mark on his destiny. There eventually came a time when his enormous success overshadowed—and even excused—his drug habits. "It's okay, it's Thelonious Monk, the great jazz pianist." But as soon as one demon was laid to rest, another raised its head. Now his mind would pay the price for his addiction, to the point where no one knew anymore *what* drug to give him for relief.

Did drugs trigger Monk's mental problems? Or did they act as a bandage for the ever-widening wound which was forcing him into total isolation? Who could possibly know? And then, what role did his bitterness play in his withdrawal from the world? The bitterness of being black, and therefore considered a second-class citizen. The bitterness of having remained misunderstood for too long by a world which thrived on ready-made truths and dissembled lies. Of having been forced to lead the life of the itinerant artist, from one town to the next like a trained bear, in conditions which became increasingly worse, until his strength was finally sapped. Of having been dropped by his last record company which, instead of carefully managing the affairs of this great artist, had squeezed him like a lemon, then cast him aside. He would have lived an intense, magnificent, and exhausting life right up to the end. After all, why should you have to die on the job? It is perfectly understandable that he needed rest.

Yet there was to be no rest. Once deprived of that vast, vital eagerness and appetite for life which had illumined his path, he was unable to resist the dark current as it swept him away. Monk was awaiting his death.

‖ 13 ‖

Death

From the beginning, Monk dwelt with death. It perched on his shoulder, like Socrates' demon, and urged him to cast farther the nets of his spirit. Death overwhelmed him and obsessed him. He saw it at work all around him, cutting down the great musical minds of the time. Charlie Christian died of tuberculosis at the age of twenty-five, like a candle that is blown out. Shadow Wilson, his favorite drummer after Art Blakey, was thrown down a subway staircase, supposedly murdered in sordid circumstances. Charlie Parker, veins scorched by poison. Billie Holiday, destroyed by pain and heartbreak. Oscar Pettiford drowned in alcohol. And then another batch a few years later: Coltrane, his liver eaten away by cancer. Bud, his brother, whose personal destiny so resembled his own. Bud, whom he encouraged in his early professional days, saying that if the kid didn't play, then he wouldn't, either. Bud, who was struck by a nightstick when he intervened between Thelonious and a cop, and was prematurely plunged into a world of suffering, dragged around from hospitals to nightclubs, then exiled to France where he struggled in vain to recover his taste for life and for music. Bud the genius, who left his mark on music as deeply as Monk did; Bud the fragile one, in his glass enclosure, who had neither the fury of Blakey, nor the arrogance of Miles. Bud, whom Monk carried to his final rest with unspeakable grief. And all his old buddies: Denzil Best, Coleman Hawkins, Elmo Hope, Joe Guy . . . And in his own family, his mother and his cousin Ronnie . . . His father, who died so nearby, without having seen him grow up . . . Death accompanied him and spoke to him. It added an essential factor to his understanding of time, and beseeched him to look it straight in the eye.

Monk was devoid of vanity, and didn't consider that tomorrow was any better or worse than today. He was haunted by the perfection of his music, and his only preoccupation was to accomplish it as fast as possible. Which he did while he was young; by the age of thirty, the die of his destiny had been cast. Time took care of the details. His close contact with death gave him a sense of detachment which never ceases to amaze. You almost get the impression that Monk saw his life constantly passing before his eyes. He had no ascendancy over his times, and waited for his music to be discovered, then suffered ten years later when it was ignored. His supreme indifference to the time of other men was an integral part of his being, and of his music. His late arrivals for concerts were legendary. But that never bothered his public, who recognized such delays as a necessity and not an insult. And when he sat down at the piano, who could ever be more *time-free*?

*　　*　　*

A jazz musician is identifiable, above all, by the way he expresses time in his music. He broadcasts a personal pulse which is recognizable amid a thousand others. McCoy Tyner is on top of the time, Hank Jones is right on it, Herbie Hancock is inside it, Dexter Gordon is behind it. But Monk is everywhere at the same time. His mastery of time is such that he seems to be emancipated from it. And the silence that he uses with such finesse is not really the suspension of time, as it is for that other master of understatement, Ahmad Jamal, nor the supreme and minimal form of elegance it is for Basie. On the contrary, it is a necessity which dazzles the ear. No, this silence is only a portion of his total music, all the more striking because it is unique. It is a creative tool, a sort of audible and quantifiable phenomenon which is a sign of a much rarer and riskier enterprise: that of *inventing* time. Saxophonist Wayne Shorter so accurately said that when you listen to a record at home, the music furnishes the room and occupies space as effectively as a staircase or a lamp. I would add that when you put a Monk record on, time itself stops in the room and becomes remodeled in his hands.

But this essential game has a price—that of defying death. Being on such intimate terms with time, could Monk have avoided relentlessly contemplating the depths of his own oblivion? Time and death are inseparably linked, and one cannot be conceived of without the other. For what is a duration if it is not finite? And an end is only an end if it brings a duration to a finish. Yes, I can hear death in Monk's music, but not with macabre colors. On the contrary, I hear it as an ancient, primitive, and powerful dialogue . . . a form of the eternal combat, fought hand-to-hand at each instant, whose stakes fade and are renewed constantly. In Monk I can see a long line of spirits of which he is the imposing reincarnation. As man-statue, he seems to contemplate both the past and the future with the certitude that his destiny was sealed milleniums ago. His family is the world, and its history, and his life binds him to this mystery. And when, exhausted by this battle, he gave up without winning the fight, then death tightened its grip and slowly suffocated him.

Shut away at the home of the Baroness, Monk took an infinite time to die. Caught in the most ancient and terrifying dialogue a man can experience, he seemed to be released from time; as if each hour spent in the silence of his room weighed either a second or a century. Aided by his wife and visited by his children, six years passed waiting for the end to come. Six years in bed, in a chair, standing by the door, in a state of total indifference to the world around him. Barry Harris, who at the time also was hospitably received by Nica, still recalls the terrible density of Thelonious, a density whose power spread like a black hole in which thousands of stars sank, one after the other. It is told that even sitting still and silent in a room, he could close a door twenty feet away without lifting a finger. And, very rarely, you could hear the piano resound to the chords of "What Is This Thing Called Love," or "My Ideal." Then Monk drew the blinds of his silence, and haunted the whole house by his mere presence.

At the end of the 1970s, should you have been invited to dinner at Nica's, you would be tempted to climb the few stairs which lead to the room where someone was being buried alive. Opening the door, you would make out the figure of someone standing there, turning his back on you. From the window, you could see the bright lights of New York City. The space of the room, which casts a pall on any living thing, suddenly would turn as hard as concrete. Fifty melodies would begin to squeal in the darkness, a terrifying din forced into absolute silence. Each gesture would become perilous and vital. From the bottom of the stairs, the sound of conversation would reach this tomb like a stretched wire, straining to snap. You would hope to see this shadow make even the tiniest movement, but it would remain motionless, and mineral.

Prompted by a final breath, you would close the door.

Thelonious Monk died of a cerebral hemorrhage on February 17, 1982.